5-INGREDIENT SMOOTHIE RECIPE BOOK

5-INGREDIENT
Smoothie Recipe Book

100 Nutrient-Packed Smoothies

AMY GONZALEZ, RD, FNTP

Photography by Laura Flippen

ROCKRIDGE
PRESS

For general information on our other products and services or to obtain technical support, please contact our Customer Care Department within the United States at (866) 744-2665, or outside the United States at (510) 253-0500.

Rockridge Press publishes its books in a variety of electronic and print formats. Some content that appears in print may not be available in electronic books, and vice versa.

Interior and Cover Designer: Mando Daniel

Art Producer: Janice Ackerman

Editor: Van Van Cleave

Photography: © 2021 Laura Flippen

Author Photo: Courtesy of Lindsay Klatzkin.

ISBN: Print 978-1-64876-620-6 | eBook 978-1-64876-119-5

R0

Dedicated to my boys—the reason
behind everything I do.

Contents

Introduction

When I was a teenager, I struggled with acne. I tried every skin care product under the sun, and still new pimples popped up almost every day. I hid them under layers of makeup and my self-esteem suffered. Along with the acne, I experienced intense sugar cravings. I would sneak sweets (especially chocolate) whenever I could. I'm not sure how much sugar I was consuming, but in hindsight, it was surely more than I would care to admit. I also grew up during the "low-fat" era and was afraid of fats—even wholesome and nourishing ones. Though I didn't know it at the time, these dietary gaps set me up for skin problems.

Flash forward to my first day of college. I enrolled in an introduction to nutrition class and promptly switched my major. I was fascinated to learn the symptoms associated with nutritional deficiencies, and how even a marginal deficiency could cause nagging issues. Later on, as I continued my education in functional nutrition, I came to look at conditions such as my acne—which I was told was simply "genetic"—as symptoms of larger nutritional problems. Those symptoms were my body's way of telling me something was off balance! I committed myself to using food as a source of healing.

However, once I entered the working world, I was frustrated to find that the diet I was supposed to put my clients on was the generic "one-size-fits-all" governmental guideline, rather than a more personalized approach. I noticed my clients suffering from conditions such as allergies, eczema, and diabetes, and while I recognized that nutritional intervention could help, the generic guidelines were not enough. Individual problems needed individualized solutions. Take my stubborn acne: eventually I learned that it was likely related to poor gut health, lack of healthy fats, and imbalanced blood sugar. My teenage self was shocked: my body had been trying to tell me something all along!

Now I like to take the same personalized approach with my clients: What is bothering you? How can changing your diet help? What nutrients do you truly need? The answer to their problems almost always begins with a whole foods nutritional philosophy. This philosophy teaches that the body works optimally when you cut the sugar, refined grains, and processed foods, and focus on consuming properly raised meats, quality fats, and colorful vegetables and fruits. In following this approach, my clients have experienced radical changes in their own health, overcoming debilitating stomach pain, skin issues, migraines, and more.

Still, many people find a whole foods diet intimidating. Thankfully, smoothies are an epiphany in easily eating well. They are fast to prepare, take almost no cooking skills, and require just a few nutrient-dense ingredients. But what you put in your smoothie matters. Many people think of the heavily fruit juice–laden smoothies as "healthy," but they can be doing more harm than good. I'll admit, my husband and I were guilty of drinking these sugar bombs early in our marriage (which didn't help with my acne), but we long ago moved toward more balanced, vegetable-driven smoothies. As a result, I felt more satiated, experienced greater mental clarity, and have better digestion. Plus, that pesky acne finally cleared up for good! With the help of smoothies, I finally felt like myself again, and that was truly revolutionary.

So, look no further to kick-start your own whole foods journey. Healthy eating does not mean a complete diet overhaul or long hours in the kitchen; something as simple as implementing a daily smoothie is a quick way to boost your nutrients. This book is full of nutritionally balanced smoothies made with a handful of familiar, easy-to-find ingredients. Each chapter is organized to help you with a specific need—whether that's refueling after a workout or satisfying your sweet tooth—and every smoothie was crafted thoughtfully so that you can personalize your diet to rectify your own nutritional gaps. These smoothies worked wonders for my health, and I hope they'll do the same for you.

CHAPTER 1

BLEND YOUR WAY TO BETTER HEALTH

When I first started making smoothies, I had a lot more flops than tasty creations, like brown, murky smoothies that were flavorless or others that were way too bitter. Once, when my blender wasn't working correctly, the greens didn't blend enough, and I ended up with something more like a chopped salad than a smoothie. My smoothie-making journey wasn't always, well, smooth.

I know you're eager to hit the blender, but before you begin, let's cover some of the fundamentals of smoothie-making. Failed smoothies can lead to frustration and messy kitchens, not to mention wasted food and money. Fortunately, you can learn from my kitchen failures and save yourself the pain of producing a muddy, unappetizing drink.

While creating a smoothie isn't necessarily rocket science, there are some tricks and considerations to keep in mind. In this chapter, I'll share key tips I've learned over the years from incorporating nourishing smoothies into my family's daily life. Before you know it, you, too, will become a smoothie-making expert! I'll explain why the 5-ingredient approach is ideal for smoothies, talk about the anatomy of a perfect smoothie, share best practices for a smoothie-savvy lifestyle, and give a preview of the recipes to come.

Why 5-Ingredients or Less Is More

I would argue that smoothie-making is its own kind of art. A smoothie must have a *smooth* consistency perfect for sipping—hence, the name! It needs to be the correct temperature (so you don't get brain freeze). Finally, the flavors need to be balanced and not muddied. We've all had a smoothie with way too many ingredients. Often, it comes out tasting like sludge. For this reason, when it comes to smoothies, the 5-ingredient approach is the way to go.

Now, I know it's tempting to cram more ingredients into your blender, but this isn't necessarily better for your health—or your wallet! You may not only end up spending more money but also taxing your digestive tract, overwhelming your system with nutrients that won't be absorbed anyway. The better way to do a smoothie? Focus on simple, whole-food ingredients. Fewer ingredients mean you can add *intentional* ingredients that will provide nutritional value and cleaner flavors, all while saving time in the kitchen. For a quick meal or snack option, a well-balanced smoothie will support your system instead of overloading it, and that means optimal health and wellness for everyone.

If you keep it simple, smoothies have numerous benefits for your health. They support gut health and a diverse microbiome by providing essential nutrients. Adding smoothies to your diet will keep your digestion running like a well-oiled machine. A smoothie a day may really keep the doctor away!

Balance in a Blender

People define "healthy" in a multitude of ways, so before we get started, let's clarify how this book defines a smoothie's healthiness. In this case, "healthy" means nutrient-dense and nutritionally balanced. The recipes in this book rely on the ingredients that provide the most nutrition while also containing protein, fat, fiber, and complex carbohydrates. Together, these nutrients support blood sugar levels, helping you maintain consistent energy throughout the day and feel fuller longer. Let's discuss each of these nutrients and what role they play in your smoothie.

PROTEIN is the building block of muscles, neurotransmitters, and hormones. It takes longer for the body to digest, so it keeps you feeling full longer. Some key sources of protein you'll see in these recipes include dairy, nuts, and seeds.

FATS provide long-burning sources of energy for the body, thereby keeping you satiated longer. Fat also decreases sugar cravings and improves hormone health and brain function. In these recipes, fats will come from avocados, dairy, nuts, seeds, and coconut.

COMPLEX CARBOHYDRATES provide a quick-burning source of fuel for the body and are full of vitamins, minerals, phytochemicals, and fiber. Some examples of complex carbohydrates you'll see in these recipes include fruit, vegetables, and oats.

FIBER helps provide satiety, feeds the good bacteria in the gut, and keeps you regular. Vegetables, fruits, nuts, and seeds provide the fiber in these recipes.

Whether you are enjoying a smoothie as a snack or meal, you can rest assured that all the recipes in this book are nutritionally balanced to help you avoid blood sugar crashes. The snack smoothies contain roughly 200 to 300 calories per serving and are meant to be used between meals or as tasty treats. The meal replacement smoothies trend around 400 to 700 calories and can be used in a pinch to keep you satisfied until your next meal.

Anatomy of a Healthy Smoothie

In this section, I will share my time-tested formula for the perfect smoothie. I'll cover its fundamentals, including base ingredients, blending agents, and binding agents. Even if you're already a smoothie connoisseur, be sure to read this section carefully because the examples of ingredients in each section will help further explain what this book defines as healthy. Furthermore, by following this simple formula, you will be able to customize your own smoothie concoctions and feel more confident behind the blender.

Base Ingredients

Base ingredients are the primary building blocks of your smoothie, providing much of the bulk and flavor base. Here are some of the base ingredients you'll see in these recipes:

FRUIT: Lower-glycemic fruits, such as berries, citrus fruits, and cherries, make excellent choices when you're watching your blood sugar. Fruits such as mangos, pineapple, and apples have bold, sweet flavors that can mask more earthy or bitter tastes from vegetables. Dates and other dried fruits can be used to add sweetness, but they will also add more sugar. Aim to use at least one fruit, or about a half to one cup per serving, in your smoothie. Sometimes, half the fun is coming up with creative flavor combinations!

VEGETABLES: Dark, leafy greens such as spinach, kale, dandelion greens, and Swiss chard are easy to pack into smoothies. Spinach has a milder flavor, so I suggest it often as a great starter green. Other less common vegetables, such as cauliflower, celery, carrots, zucchini, and even sweet potato can add surprising variety to your smoothies. To bring in more unique flavor profiles, you can also use herbs, such as mint, basil, sage, and cilantro. With both fruits and vegetables, it's best to choose what is available seasonally and buy organic when possible. Ideally, you'll want your smoothie to be at least half vegetables, about one to two cups per serving. If you are new to using vegetables in your smoothie, try starting with a half cup and working your way up.

SUPERFOODS: These power-packed foods can add a bit of jazz to your smoothie. Chia seeds, hemp seeds, coconut flakes, nuts, oats, cacao, and spices bring additional health benefits and flavor complexity. They appear often in the Dessert Smoothie section (see page 109).

Blending Agents

Next, you will need a liquid to blend the ingredients. Expect to use about one cup of liquid for every serving in your smoothie. This may vary depending on the ingredients you are using. For example, you may find you need less liquid if you are using fresh produce versus frozen. I recommend starting with about half to three-quarters of a cup of liquid per serving and increasing gradually as you blend until you reach your desired consistency. Here are the most common blending agents you'll see throughout this book.

WATER: While using water may seem boring, it can be an economical blending agent that does not affect the taste of your smoothie. In fact, I prefer using water in Anti-Inflammatory Mango (page 19) and Vanilla-Blackberry-Sage (page 22) because it lightens things up without sacrificing taste.

MILK: Cow's milk, goat's milk, and nondairy alternatives like almond, cashew, and coconut milk will increase your smoothie's creaminess. Kefir, a fermented milk product, makes an appearance in a few of the recipes in this book, like in Blueberry-Almond (page 37). Because of its slight effervescence, this tangy milk product brings in a slightly foamy texture. So fun to drink!

COCONUT WATER: Harvested from young coconuts, this clear liquid can add a subtle sweetness to your smoothie. Its natural electrolytes make it a great addition to post-workout recovery smoothies. Energizing Electrolytes (page 42) is one of my favorites.

BONE BROTH: Whether you're sick or just in need of a nutrient boost, bone broth is a great option. For centuries, people have boiled down the bones of healthy animals with vegetables, herbs, and spices for a variety of easily absorbable vitamins and minerals. Don't be put off by the idea of using this ingredient in your smoothie! Flavorful fruits will mask the taste, like in Fruity Bone Broth Refresher (page 50). If you're vegetarian, you can use vegetable broth or another blending agent instead.

OTHER LIQUIDS: If you'd like to get creative, you can also add coffee or brewed and chilled tea, such as green tea or hibiscus, to bring some depth to your smoothie. Check out Strawberry-Hibiscus (page 21) for a delicious example!

Binding Agents

Binding agents thicken and hold your smoothie together, preventing it from separating. Here are the most common binding agents you'll see in this book:

AVOCADO: This delicious fruit provides healthy fat, antioxidants, fiber, minerals, and vitamins while also bringing a velvety texture to your smoothie. Berry-Chocolate (page 81) is an extra-luxurious example of what an avocado can do for your smoothie! If you don't like the taste of avocados, don't worry; it's easily covered by other fruit. Use half to a whole avocado per serving of smoothie.

FROZEN BANANA: I always keep peeled bananas in my freezer for quick, creamy smoothies. Unripe bananas are mostly resistant starch, which functions similarly to soluble fiber. During ripening, the starch converts to sugar, so ripe bananas will be more naturally sweet. Banana-based smoothies, like Banana-Zucchini Bread (page 120), are fantastic for kids. Use half to one whole banana per serving.

YOGURT: Yogurt offers a thick and creamy texture. Look for full-fat plain yogurts, which are lower in sugar than flavored yogurts, or Greek yogurt if you want more protein. I probably make Superfood Supreme (page 67) at least once a week! For nondairy options, use plant-based yogurts, such as those made from coconut and almond milk. I suggest using a half cup per serving.

NUT BUTTERS: Nut butters add creaminess and lots of plant-based protein and fat. There are many options on the market today, including almond, cashew, sunflower seed, and even walnut and pecan. I tend to be more of an almond type of person, so the Cardamom-Chia Smoothie Bowl (page 68) is my go-to when I want something savory. Just be sure to choose a nut butter that does not include added sugar. Add one to two tablespoons per serving.

COTTAGE CHEESE: For those who tolerate dairy, cottage cheese adds about 13 grams of protein in a half cup serving. Don't be put off by the curds; they'll be blended up with the rest of the smoothie. I have found that cottage cheese also creates a thicker texture for a delectable, indulgent smoothie like in Strawberry Cheesecake (page 111). Use a half cup of cottage cheese per serving.

TIPS TO SAVE TIME AND MONEY

Aren't we all looking to save a minute or a dollar? Read the tips below to keep your smoothie-making fast and affordable, without sacrificing health or taste.

KEEP ON HAND: Make smoothies a daily habit by keeping the basic ingredients in your refrigerator and pantry.

MINIMIZE CLEANUP: Don't stress over having perfect measurements for your smoothies. Once you get the hang of how much of each ingredient should go in your recipe, skip the measuring cups and eyeball your measurements.

PREP AHEAD: Pre-portion what you need for your smoothie by tossing your fruit, vegetables, and powders in a freezer-safe bag. Store the bag in the freezer, then when you're ready to blend, simply add liquid and go!

WASH AND FREEZE: Leafy greens can be washed, dried, and frozen to keep them fresh longer.

DOUBLE IT: To minimize the amount of time you're blending, double a batch of your smoothie. Simply add a lid and save in the refrigerator for the next day. Your smoothie will have the best nutrition within 24 hours. Just give it a quick blend before drinking.

FREEZE CREATIVELY: Use ice cube trays to freeze dairy; chopped produce such as herbs, greens, and fruit; and other ingredients that are about to expire or spoil.

REFRIGERATE IT: Nuts, seeds, and their butters last longer and retain more of their nutrients when refrigerated.

BUY FROZEN: Opt for frozen produce when available. Frozen fruits and vegetables are picked at the peak of ripeness, will be more nutrient-dense, and will last longer. Plus, they provide a thick texture to smoothies, eliminating the need for ice, which waters down your smoothies.

SHOP SEASONALLY: When shopping for fresh produce, choose in-season fruits and vegetables to save money.

CATCH THE SALES: Whenever you see fruits and vegetables on sale, stock up. Then, just wash, portion, and freeze for future use.

Tools of the Trade

Now that you know the foundational ingredients for a delicious smoothie, you'll need to know how to put them together. The good news is that it's as easy as you think! With just a handful of tools and minimal prep, you will be enjoying a satisfying beverage in no time. Let's highlight some of the equipment that you will need to pull off the recipes in this book.

BLENDER: This is the most important tool you'll need to make your smoothie. Because there are a wide range of blenders on the market, it can be overwhelming to know what qualities are important. When assessing appliances, you'll want to consider power, durability, ease of cleaning, and size. Choosing a powerful motor is important when you'll be using the blender to puree nuts, seeds, and frozen fruit. A weak motor can cause chunky and less-than-desirable smoothies. Frozen fruits especially can be tough on the blender, so be sure to choose a high-powered version with a stainless-steel blade, which is the most durable. The size of blender containers varies widely, ranging from personal size (12 to 16 ounces) to 72 ounces. Use whatever works best for you. The recipes in this book were all made using a 48-ounce blender.

SHARP KNIFE: A chef's knife is ideal for chopping fruits and vegetables into smaller chunks before tossing them into your blender. Smaller chunks will allow you to fit more into your blender and will be easier on the motor. Knives should always be washed by hand and sharpened regularly. Remember, a dull blade is more dangerous than a sharp one.

CUTTING BOARD: A sturdy cutting board is helpful when chopping fruits and vegetables. I prefer one made from bamboo since it's naturally antimicrobial.

LIDDED GLASS JARS: Glass jars that have lids are great for drinking, transporting, and saving your smoothie.

MEASURING CUPS: Both a liquid measuring cup and a set of dry measuring cups are helpful for measuring your smoothie ingredients. Yes, there is a difference!

Smooth Operator

Help! Did your smoothie turn out less than ideal? Sometimes, a smoothie can be saved with a little troubleshooting, so read my hacks below before tossing it.

Problem: My smoothie is too thick.

Solution: This is a simple fix. Add more liquid. I suggest using the same liquid you used in the recipe, but water can be used as well.

Problem: My smoothie is too thin.

Solution: To salvage a thin smoothie, try adding a thickener, such as banana, avocado, frozen fruit, nut butter, or chia seeds. And next time, try freezing your ingredients or using less liquid.

Problem: My smoothie is too grainy.

Solution: First, check your blender. Ensure the motor and blades are working properly and in good condition. For a low-powered blender, you may need to blend your greens and liquid first. Then, add the remaining ingredients and blend until smooth. You can also add additional binding agents, such as avocados, banana, or yogurt, to increase the creaminess.

Problem: I have leftovers.

Solution: Put a lid on your cup and save it in the refrigerator for later. It's best to consume a smoothie within 24 hours—any longer, and it loses a lot of its nutrition. You can also freeze a smoothie in an airtight container for up to three months or even make it into popsicles!

Problem: My smoothie is too bitter.

Solution: If you need to sweeten your smoothie, try increasing the quantity of fruit to keep the sugar content low. If that's still not enough, add a touch of honey or use coconut water as the liquid. A little goes a long way with sweeteners, so keep a steady hand. Once your taste buds adjust, you can slowly back away from these additional ingredients.

HIDDEN HEALTH GEMS

In the coming recipes, you may find some "unusual" (but easy to find!) ingredients that you may never have considered putting in a smoothie. These ingredients are nutrient-packed and delicious, so I suggest you give them a go. Below, I'll explain what some of these ingredients are and why they work.

MATCHA POWDER: This green tea powder is packed with antioxidants and gives an energy boost to your day. It pairs well with fruit in green smoothies.

CINNAMON: This spice adds a natural sweetness without any sugar. Try using other spices, such as nutmeg and turmeric, to deepen your smoothie's flavor.

HEMP SEEDS: These provide a plant-based source of protein and add a creamy texture to smoothies. You can even use them as a garnish on top!

CHIA SEEDS: These little black seeds are packed with healthy fat, protein, and fiber. They absorb moisture and contribute to a thicker smoothie.

GRASS-FED COLLAGEN POWDER: Collagen provides a quick protein source to smoothies without affecting the flavor. Just remember that it's not vegetarian!

FROZEN AND STEAMED BUTTERNUT SQUASH: This vegetable brings a mild sweetness to your smoothie, along with fiber, vitamin A, and vitamin C.

ROLLED OATS: Oats are an easy-to-find ingredient that add fiber and protein to your smoothie, keeping you fuller longer. Note that rolled oats are easier to blend than other types.

Before You Blend

Whew! We've just about covered all the basics of smoothie prep, and you're likely anxious to get started. But before you do, let me tell you a little bit about the recipes to come.

As you scan through the following pages, you'll notice a few key traits of each recipe. First, no recipe calls for more than five ingredients, excluding common household ingredients such as water, ice, and salt. While some smoothies are meant to be quick snacks and others meal replacements, all use five ingredients or fewer and are nutritionally balanced—yes, even the dessert smoothies!

Secondly, every recipe is designed to make two (12- to 16-ounce) servings. If you have leftovers, just put a lid on your smoothie, refrigerate it for up to 24 hours, and quickly re-blend it before enjoying.

And lastly, every recipe will include a tip to help customize your smoothie to your liking. This way, your smoothie comes out exactly how *you* like it!

- **Health Hack** helps you make the recipe even healthier

- **Simplify** makes the recipe easier or quicker

- **Substitute** tells you how to replace an ingredient

- **Supercharge** lets you add an ingredient to maximize nutrition

- **Kid Friendly** helps you make the recipe palatable for children

As you begin your smoothie journey, don't forget that *how* you eat your smoothie is just as important as what you put in it. Digestion starts in the brain. The simple act of slowing down to chew rather than slurp your smoothie can activate the digestive process. While it may sound silly, chewing your smoothie can be the best thing you do for your body to help it gear up for the wonderful nutrition that's about to come.

All right. Are you ready? Go grab your blender!

SIPPABLE SNACKS

Antioxidant Ruby-Red

Beets are often an undercelebrated vegetable, but this should not be the case! They are packed with vitamins, minerals, and antioxidants that provide anti-inflammatory benefits and support detoxification. They also give this smoothie a cheery, vibrant ruby-red color that will pick you up any day.

½ cup frozen pitted cherries
¼ cup frozen blueberries
¼ cup frozen blackberries
½ cup chopped red beets
½ cup full-fat plain Greek yogurt
1½ cups water

MAKES 2 (14-ounce) servings
PREP TIME 5 minutes

1. Put the cherries, blueberries, blackberries, beets, yogurt, and water in a blender. Blend on high speed until smooth.
2. Divide evenly between 2 cups and enjoy!

SUBSTITUTE Use any mix of berries totaling 1 cup. You can also substitute any nondairy yogurt alternative for the Greek yogurt.

Per serving: Calories: 207; Total Fat: 6.9g; Sugars: 16.6g; Carbohydrates: 23.4g; Fiber: 6.1g; Protein: 12.5g; Sodium: 102mg

Blue Blast

The first time I added radishes to my smoothie, I wasn't quite sure what to expect. However, I was pleasantly surprised with the result! The radishes bring in a slight peppery edge to complement the natural sweetness of the fruit. Radishes are mostly water but are also chock-full of fiber, vitamin C, B vitamins, and antioxidants, enriching this smoothie with robust flavor and nutrition.

1 cup frozen blueberries

1 pear, chopped

1 banana, halved and frozen

1 cup chopped radishes

1½ cups unsweetened almond milk

1. Put the blueberries, pear, banana, radishes, and almond milk in a blender. Blend on high speed until smooth.

2. Divide evenly between 2 cups and enjoy!

Per serving: Calories: 153; Total Fat: 3.1g; Sugars: 19.1g; Carbohydrates: 32.2g; Fiber: 7.5g; Protein: 2.4g; Sodium: 144mg

MAKES 2 (14-ounce) servings

PREP TIME 5 minutes

HEALTH HACK To increase the protein and make a more satiating smoothie, add 1 cup of full-fat plain yogurt.

Tart Cherry Limeade Slushie

Pucker up! This cherry limeade smoothie comes with a sour punch and will leave you feeling refreshed. The coconut water will help keep you hydrated and provide a natural sweetness. Just be sure to use 100 percent pure coconut water with no added sugars.

1 cup frozen pitted cherries

1 lime, peeled

½ cup fresh spinach

½ cup chopped cucumber

1½ cups coconut water

1. Put the cherries, lime, spinach, cucumber, and coconut water in a blender. Blend on high speed until smooth.
2. Divide evenly between 2 cups and enjoy!

Per serving: Calories: 86; Total Fat: 0.8g; Sugars: 12.7g; Carbohydrates: 20g; Fiber: 4.3g; Protein: 2.6g; Sodium: 209mg

MAKES 2 (12-ounce) servings

PREP TIME 5 minutes

HEALTH HACK Before peeling your lime, collect the zest. Wash the lime first, then zest it using a small grater or zester. Use this zest in this smoothie for extra tartness or freeze it for later.

Anti-Inflammatory Mango

Turmeric is the star in this smoothie for its anti-inflammatory properties. This root's benefits are primarily derived from its active compound, curcumin, which has been shown to be more effective than common anti-inflammatory medications. The turmeric and mango also give this smoothie its bright, golden color.

1 cup frozen mango chunks

1 cup frozen cauliflower florets

2 teaspoons ground turmeric

2 tablespoons ground flaxseed

1 cup full-fat plain Greek yogurt

1½ cups water

1. Put the mango, cauliflower, turmeric, flaxseed, yogurt, and water in a blender. Blend on high speed until smooth.

2. Divide evenly between 2 cups and enjoy!

Per serving: Calories: 222; Total Fat: 9.6g; Sugars: 13.6g; Carbohydrates: 20.9g; Fiber: 5.4g; Protein: 13g; Sodium: 67.5mg

MAKES 2 (16-ounce) servings

PREP TIME 5 minutes

SUBSTITUTE Cauliflower is used in this recipe since it's easy to disguise its neutral taste and doesn't affect this smoothie's vibrant golden color. However, if you'd like an alternative, try using spinach or zucchini.

Zinc Defense

Looking to boost your immune system? Spinach, pumpkin seeds, and kefir are great sources of zinc, which performs hundreds of functions in the body, including activation of the immune system. Zinc is also involved in healing the skin, activating enzymes, balancing hormones, making proteins, and synthesizing DNA.

½ cup frozen sliced peaches

½ cup frozen pineapple chunks

1 cup fresh spinach

½ cup pumpkin seeds

1 cup plain kefir

½ cup water

1. Put the peaches, pineapple, spinach, pumpkin seeds, kefir, and water in a blender. Blend on high speed until smooth.
2. Divide evenly between 2 cups and enjoy!

Per serving: Calories: 186; Total Fat: 7.3g; Sugars: 13.3g; Carbohydrates: 24.5g; Fiber: 1.2g; Protein: 8g; Sodium: 99.7mg

MAKES 2 (14-ounce) servings
PREP TIME 5 minutes

SIMPLIFY Reduce food waste by freezing fresh greens before they wilt. Simply wash, chop, and let them air dry. Once they are completely dry, store them in a freezer-safe container to use in smoothies, soups, and other recipes.

Strawberry-Hibiscus

This smoothie uses hibiscus tea as its liquid blending agent. Chilled teas make wonderful additions to smoothies, as they provide subtle flavor undertones. Hibiscus has a naturally tart taste, so if you need to sweeten the smoothie, try adding extra berries or a dab of honey.

1 tablespoon dried hibiscus flowers

½ cup boiling water

1 cup frozen strawberries

1 banana, halved and frozen

1 cup chopped cauliflower

1 cup coconut water

MAKES 2 (16-ounce) servings

PREP TIME 10 minutes

1. Steep the hibiscus flowers in the boiling water for 5 minutes. Allow the tea to cool to room temperature, without removing the hibiscus flowers. Alternatively, you can prepare the tea ahead of time and chill it in the refrigerator for up to 5 days.

2. Once the tea is cooled, pour the tea with the soaked hibiscus flowers, strawberries, banana, cauliflower, and coconut water into a blender. Blend on high speed until smooth.

3. Divide evenly between 2 cups and enjoy!

SIMPLIFY Next time you make tea to drink, make some extra and freeze it in an ice cube tray for smoothies later. Green, black, and herbal teas bring unique flavor profiles to smoothies.

Per serving: Calories: 128; Total Fat: 0.9g; Sugars: 16.6g; Carbohydrates: 30.1g; Fiber: 7.6g; Protein: 3.4g; Sodium: 143mg

Vanilla-Blackberry-Sage

This was the first smoothie in which I used sage. I had used the more common herbs, such as mint and basil, in my smoothies, but sage was not one of my typical go-tos. Once I tried it, I was kicking myself for not trying it sooner. This savory herb plays up the deep flavors of blackberry and vanilla. Soon, you'll be finding more ways to incorporate sage in your smoothies, too!

1 cup frozen blackberries

1 cup chopped chard

½ cup raw cashews

1 teaspoon vanilla extract

6 fresh sage leaves

1½ cups water

MAKES 2 (16-ounce) servings

PREP TIME 5 minutes

1. Put the blackberries, chard, cashews, vanilla, sage, and water in a blender. Blend on high speed until smooth.

2. Divide evenly between 2 cups and enjoy!

Per serving: Calories: 196; Total Fat: 12.7g; Sugars: 5.6g; Carbohydrates: 17.6g; Fiber: 5.1g; Protein: 6.5g; Sodium: 42.6mg

HEALTH HACK For an even silkier texture, try soaking the cashews in water overnight. This will also increase the digestibility of the nuts.

Tropical Matcha

If you're looking for a pick-me-up, this smoothie may be just what you need. While the history of green tea in China dates to around the seventh to tenth centuries, the process of making powdered teas from pulverized, steam-dried leaves began around the tenth to thirteenth centuries. Matcha became a part of Zen Buddhists' daily ritual to improve their meditative states. We now know that this benefit comes from the combination of the caffeine and L-theanine. Once ground, matcha oxidizes quickly. Store ground matcha in a cool, dark place to keep it fresh for up to a few months.

½ cup frozen papaya chunks

½ cup frozen mango chunks

1 cup chopped kale

2 teaspoons matcha powder

1 avocado, peeled and pitted

1½ cups water

1. Put the papaya, mango, kale, matcha powder, avocado, and water in a blender. Blend on high speed until smooth.
2. Divide evenly between 2 cups and enjoy!

Per serving: Calories: 218; Total Fat: 15.1g; Sugars: 8.8g; Carbohydrates: 22.4g; Fiber: 8.8g; Protein: 3.5g; Sodium: 23.3mg

MAKES 2 (12-ounce) servings

PREP TIME 5 minutes

SUBSTITUTE If you don't have matcha, try swapping the matcha powder and water for chilled green tea instead.

Sippable Snacks

ABC

Apples, beets, and carrots have been the staple ingredients for slaws and juices, for their delicious taste and liver cleansing properties. Liver tonics date back from the first century for their restorative, cleansing, and protective effects. Now these three easy-to-remember ingredients come together in smoothie form to create a nutritional powerhouse that supports the detoxification process.

1 green apple, chopped and frozen

½ cup chopped red beets, frozen

1 cup chopped carrots

1 (1-inch) piece ginger, sliced

1½ cups unsweetened almond milk

1. Put the apple, beets, carrots, ginger, and almond milk in a blender. Blend on high speed until smooth.
2. Divide evenly between 2 cups and enjoy!

Per serving: Calories: 103; Total Fat: 2.5g; Sugars: 13.3g; Carbohydrates: 20g; Fiber: 4.9g; Protein: 1.8g; Sodium: 172mg

MAKES 2 (12-ounce) servings

PREP TIME 5 minutes

SIMPLIFY Don't throw away the leafy greens from the beets! Save them to use in other smoothies, such as Blueberry-Almond (page 37).

Vitamin C Punch

Studies show that 100 to 200 milligrams of vitamin C per day is best for pro-phylactic prevention of infection and reducing the severity and duration of cold symptoms. However, since vitamin C is water-soluble, your body will excrete what it does not need. Offering 276 milligrams of vitamin C, this smoothie is way better for you than those vitamin C packets you pick up in the grocery store checkout.

1 medium orange, peeled

1 cup chopped, seeded guava, frozen

½ cup diced jicama

1 cup chopped kale

1 cup plain kefir

½ cup water

1. Put the orange, guava, jicama, kale, kefir, and water in a blender. Blend on high speed until smooth.

2. Divide evenly between 2 cups and enjoy!

Per serving: Calories: 194; Total Fat: 5.2g; Sugars: 19.8g; Carbohydrates: 32.6g; Fiber: 8.1g; Protein: 8.1g; Sodium: 78mg

MAKES 2 (16-ounce) servings

PREP TIME 5 minutes

KID FRIENDLY If your family is new to using greens in smoothies, try starting with spinach, which has a milder taste than kale.

Berry-Basil

It may seem unusual using herbs in smoothies, but they can bring new life to your beverages and keep things interesting. Basil, with its light, earthy taste, pairs well with most fruits. We're using mixed berries here, but if you're looking to mix things up, try using mango, strawberries, or peach instead.

1 cup frozen mixed berries

1 cup chopped chard

¼ cup lightly packed fresh basil

1 tablespoon chia seeds

1½ cups unsweetened almond milk

MAKES 2 (14-ounce) servings

PREP TIME 5 minutes

1. Put the berries, chard, basil, chia seeds, and almond milk in a blender. Blend on high speed until smooth.

2. Divide evenly between 2 cups and enjoy!

Per serving: Calories: 212; Total Fat: 11.5g; Sugars: 7.8g; Carbohydrates: 23.9g; Fiber: 13.1g; Protein: 6.6g; Sodium: 322mg

HEALTH HACK Adding 3 tablespoons of nut butter will increase the smoothie's creaminess and protein content (about 6 grams per serving).

Citrus Crush

When oranges and grapefruit are in season, we typically buy 20-pound bags from our local farmer. So that we don't get bored by the time we get to the bottom of the bag, we use them in smoothies. I found the lively trio of oranges, grapefruit, and pineapple paired with the creamy coconut milk to be a great way to brighten up my day. We also enjoy making larger batches of this smoothie and freezing it when we have a surplus!

1 medium orange, peeled

½ medium grapefruit, peeled

½ cup frozen pineapple chunks

½ cup chopped zucchini

½ cup coconut milk

½ cup water

MAKES 2 (16-ounce) servings

PREP TIME 5 minutes

1. Put the orange, grapefruit, pineapple, zucchini, coconut milk, and water in a blender. Blend on high speed until smooth.

2. Divide evenly between 2 cups and enjoy!

Per serving: Calories: 197; Total Fat: 12.3g; Sugars: 14.8g; Carbohydrates: 23.4g; Fiber: 3.4g; Protein: 2.8g; Sodium: 11.6mg

SUPERCHARGE Try adding the superfood bee pollen to this smoothie. Bee pollen is packed with B vitamins, minerals, free amino acids, and protein and has some incredible health benefits. It's been shown to provide allergy relief, support the immune system, and reduce inflammation.

Creamy Watermelon Mojito

Nothing says summer more than watermelon! The hydrating watermelon and cucumbers paired with the creamy yogurt make this smoothie feel like a lavish beverage—perfect for poolside sippin'. To step up the flavor, try adding some lime juice, lime zest, and even a splash of vanilla extract.

1 cup cubed watermelon, frozen

1 cup chopped cucumber, frozen

¼ cup lightly packed fresh mint leaves

1 tablespoon chia seeds

1 cup full-fat plain Greek yogurt

¾ cup water

MAKES 2 (16-ounce) servings

PREP TIME 5 minutes

1. Put the watermelon, cucumber, mint, chia seeds, yogurt, and water in a blender. Blend on high speed until smooth.
2. Divide evenly between 2 cups and enjoy!

Per serving: Calories: 191; Total Fat: 9.4g; Sugars: 5.6g; Carbohydrates: 12.8g; Fiber: 4.8g; Protein: 12.6g; Sodium: 52.2mg

SIMPLIFY Save time by keeping frozen watermelon on hand in the freezer. To freeze, first cube the watermelon and remove its seeds. Spread the watermelon evenly across a baking sheet lined with parchment or wax paper. Put the tray in the freezer until the watermelon is frozen solid, and then transfer it to a storage-safe bag.

Red, White, and Blue

Jicama, also known as yam bean, Mexican turnip, or Mexican potato, is a tuberous root native to Mexico. It is often sold by street vendors and eaten raw, seasoned with lime juice and chili powder.

½ cup frozen strawberries

1 cup chopped jicama

½ cup frozen blueberries

¼ cup almonds

1½ cups almond milk

1. Put the strawberries, jicama, blueberries, almonds, and almond milk in a blender. Blend on high speed until smooth.

2. Divide evenly between 2 cups and enjoy!

Per serving: Calories: 184; Total Fat: 11.8g; Sugars: 7.1g; Carbohydrates: 17g; Fiber: 7.5g; Protein: 5.4g; Sodium: 123mg

MAKES 2 (14-ounce) servings

PREP TIME 5 minutes

SUBSTITUTE If you are unable to find jicama, an apple or green grapes would make a great replacement.

Spicy Green

One way to instantly liven up your smoothie is to add some cayenne pepper. Keep in mind that cow's milk will dissipate the heat, so it's best to stick with plant-based milk unless you find that you've added a little too much spice. In that case, a splash of cow's milk will calm the heat.

1 pear, chopped and frozen

1 kiwi, peeled, chopped, and frozen

1 cup fresh spinach

¼ teaspoon cayenne pepper

1½ cups unsweetened almond milk

MAKES 2 (16-ounce) servings

PREP TIME 5 minutes

1. Put the pear, kiwi, spinach, cayenne pepper, and almond milk in a blender. Blend on high speed until smooth.

2. Divide evenly between 2 cups and enjoy!

Per serving: Calories: 167; Total Fat: 5.4g; Sugars: 16.8g; Carbohydrates: 29.2g; Fiber: 8.6g; Protein: 4g; Sodium: 316mg

SUBSTITUTE If you're not a fan of spicy foods, try replacing the cayenne pepper with milder flavors, such as ginger, basil, or mint.

PROTEIN-POWERED REFUEL

Tangy Raspberry Chia

Protein powders are a convenient way to boost the protein content of your smoothie. The protein source of these powders can come from animal protein (casein, whey, and collagen) or plant-based proteins (pea, hemp, and rice). When shopping for these, be sure to check the list of ingredients. Choose one with simple ingredients and no added sugar or artificial sweeteners.

1 cup frozen raspberries

2 tablespoons chia seeds

1 cup frozen cauliflower florets

2 scoops protein powder

½ cup coconut milk

½ cup water

MAKES 2 (12-ounce) servings

PREP TIME 5 minutes

1. Put the raspberries, chia seeds, cauliflower, protein powder, coconut milk, and water in a blender. Blend on high speed until smooth.

2. Divide evenly between 2 cups and enjoy!

Per serving: Calories: 302; Total Fat: 18.9g; Sugars: 3.9g; Carbohydrates: 19.3g; Fiber: 11.8g; Protein: 18.1g; Sodium: 48.8mg

SUPERCHARGE Add another vegetable to this smoothie by tossing in a handful of spinach; round out the flavor with some additional raspberries.

Peanut Butter Cup

Craving a peanut butter cup? Satisfy that craving without the guilt! This smoothie is one of my personal favorites for a sweet fix. The ingredients are easy to keep on hand, and I love that I can offer my kids a healthy chocolate shake alternative that won't crash their blood sugar.

**2 bananas, halved
   and frozen**
**2 tablespoons
   collagen powder**
**2 tablespoons raw
   cacao powder**

¼ cup peanut butter
**1½ cups unsweetened
   almond milk**

MAKES 2 (12-ounce)
servings
PREP TIME 5 minutes

SUPERCHARGE Add
some maca powder to this
smoothie to give it a chocolate malt taste while also
offering hormone-balancing
support.

1. Put the bananas, collagen powder, cacao powder, peanut butter, and almond milk in a blender. Blend on high speed until smooth.

2. Divide evenly between 2 cups and enjoy!

Per serving: Calories: 368; Total Fat: 19.6g; Sugars: 17.5g; Carbohydrates: 37.2g; Fiber: 7.5g; Protein: 20.2g; Sodium: 183mg

Ginger-Plum

One of the lesser-known benefits of smoothies are their impact on gut health. Fruits and vegetables contain fibers that feed our microbiome—the good bacteria living in our gut. Fermented and cultured foods, such as yogurt and kefir, contain probiotics that help populate our gut with the good guys. A happy and healthy gut means a stronger immune system, improved mood, and better digestion.

3 plums, diced and frozen

1 cup chopped kale

1 (1-inch) piece ginger, sliced

2 scoops protein powder

1 cup full-fat plain Greek yogurt

¾ cup water

1. Put the plums, kale, ginger, protein powder, yogurt, and water in a blender. Blend on high speed until smooth.

2. Divide evenly between 2 cups and enjoy!

Per serving: Calories: 220; Total Fat: 7.4g; Sugars: 9.9g; Carbohydrates: 13g; Fiber: 1.5g; Protein: 23.7g; Sodium: 107mg

MAKES 2 (14-ounce) servings

PREP TIME 5 minutes

SIMPLIFY Store ginger root in your freezer to help it last longer. When you're ready to use it, simply pull it out of the freezer and use a cheese grater to grate what you need. No need to peel it beforehand!

Blueberry-Almond

Kefir is a fermented milk product that originated in the Caucasus Mountains many centuries ago. Kefir means "pleasure drink" and is traditionally made from cow's or goat's milk. While it's like yogurt in its sourness, kefir is slightly fizzy and more drinkable. In the 1930s, it was highly popular in the Soviet Union and continues to be the cornerstone for many weight-loss diets in Russia. Kefir has tons of B vitamins, folate, and easy-to-digest proteins, making it perfect for those who are lactose intolerant.

1 cup frozen blueberries

1 cup chopped beet greens

¼ cup almonds

2 scoops protein powder

1 cup plain kefir

½ cup water

1. Put the blueberries, beet greens, almonds, protein powder, kefir, and water in a blender. Blend on high speed until smooth.

2. Divide evenly between 2 cups and enjoy!

Per serving: Calories: 282; Total Fat: 14.6g; Sugars: 13.5g; Carbohydrates: 19.6g; Fiber: 4.8g; Protein: 21.1g; Sodium: 126mg

MAKES 2 (16-ounce) servings

PREP TIME 5 minutes

SUBSTITUTE If you're unable to locate kefir, substitute full-fat plain Greek yogurt or a plant-based yogurt for a dairy-free alternative.

Protein-Powered Refuel

PB-Banana-Oat Recovery

Oats aren't just for oatmeal; they also help make a silky and satisfying smoothie! Oats are high in the soluble fiber beta-glucan, which supports heart health, digestion, and maintaining healthy gut bacteria. Offering six grams of protein per half cup, oats help bring this creamy smoothie to a total of 25 grams of protein. I've found that even after the most intense of workouts, this smoothie provides the perfect balance for a quick refuel post-workout!

2 bananas, halved and frozen

2 tablespoons peanut butter

½ cup rolled oats

2 scoops protein powder

1½ cups unsweetened almond milk

MAKES 2 (14-ounce) servings

PREP TIME 5 minutes

HEALTH HACK Try soaking your oats in the milk overnight for a creamier smoothie.

1. Put the bananas, peanut butter, oats, protein powder, and almond milk in a blender. Blend on high speed until smooth.

2. Divide evenly between 2 cups and enjoy!

Per serving: Calories: 437; Total Fat: 14.4g; Sugars: 15.9g; Carbohydrates: 56.7g; Fiber: 8.9g; Protein: 25.1g; Sodium: 147mg

Pink Passion Protein

There's something about brightly colored smoothies that makes them even more fun to drink. To make a vibrant pink, we're using red-pigmented fruits and vegetables combined with white yogurt. Lycopene gives the fruits and vegetables their red color; it also offers antioxidant properties, which helps decrease cancer risk and support heart health.

1 cup cubed
 watermelon, frozen
½ cup frozen raspberries
½ cup chopped red beets

1 cup full-fat plain
 Greek yogurt
2 scoops protein powder
¾ cup water

MAKES 2 (14-ounce) servings
PREP TIME 5 minutes

1. Put the watermelon, raspberries, beets, yogurt, protein powder, and water in a blender. Blend on high speed until smooth.
2. Divide evenly between 2 cups and enjoy!

Per serving: Calories: 220; Total Fat: 7.4g; Sugars: 8.4g; Carbohydrates: 12.7g; Fiber: 3.3g; Protein: 23.9g; Sodium: 97.6mg

SUBSTITUTE Try swapping out the watermelon, raspberries, and beets in this smoothie for any red fruits or vegetables, such as raspberries, cherries, or even tomatoes.

Strawberry, Peach, and Cottage Cheese

One of my favorite snacks as a child was a big bowl of cottage cheese with fresh peaches on top. This smoothie brings back memories from my childhood while also sneaking in a vegetable. The next time peaches are in season, be sure to stock up and freeze them. Using frozen, in-season fruit will make your smoothie even sweeter!

1 cup frozen sliced peaches

½ cup frozen strawberries

1 cup frozen cauliflower florets

¼ cup chopped walnuts

1 cup full-fat cottage cheese

1 cup water

MAKES 2 (16-ounce) servings

PREP TIME 5 minutes

1. Put the peaches, strawberries, cauliflower, walnuts, cottage cheese, and water in a blender. Blend on high speed until smooth.

2. Divide evenly between 2 cups and enjoy!

SUBSTITUTE Substitute any nuts for the walnuts. I have tried both almonds and pecans with great success.

Per serving: Calories: 253; Total Fat: 14.4g; Sugars: 12.7g; Carbohydrates: 18.7g; Fiber: 4.1g; Protein: 15.9g; Sodium: 398mg

Green Power Protein

What's better than a green smoothie? A protein-packed green smoothie! Here, we are using protein powder for the protein source, but you can replace it with hemp seeds, yogurt, or cottage cheese. For a milder flavor, try swapping the kale with spinach.

1 cup chopped kale

1 medium green apple, chopped

1 banana, halved and frozen

2 scoops protein powder

1½ cups unsweetened almond milk

MAKES 2 (12-ounce) servings

PREP TIME 5 minutes

SUPERCHARGE Add some healthy fat to this smoothie with half an avocado (7.5 grams per serving).

1. Put the kale, apple, banana, protein powder, and almond milk in a blender. Blend on high speed until smooth.

2. Divide evenly between 2 cups and enjoy!

Per serving: Calories: 203; Total Fat: 3.8g; Sugars: 16.7g; Carbohydrates: 30.1g; Fiber: 5.1g; Protein: 15.2g; Sodium: 158mg

Energizing Electrolytes

Electrolytes are minerals that our bodies use for muscle and nerve function, blood pressure maintenance, and hydration. An electrolyte imbalance caused by sweating or illness can lead to muscle cramping, headaches, and fatigue. To refuel your electrolyte stores, skip the sports drinks, which contain artificial dyes and flavors, and give this smoothie a try.

2 cups cubed watermelon, frozen

½ cup pomegranate seeds

½ cup frozen strawberries

2 scoops protein powder

¾ cup coconut water

Pinch Himalayan sea salt

1. Put the watermelon, pomegranate seeds, strawberries, protein powder, coconut water, and salt in a blender. Blend on high speed until smooth.

2. Divide evenly between 2 cups and enjoy!

Per serving: Calories: 172; Total Fat: 2g; Sugars: 19.7g; Carbohydrates: 26g; Fiber: 4.1g; Protein: 15.1g; Sodium: 120mg

MAKES 2 (14-ounce) servings

PREP TIME 5 minutes

SUPERCHARGE To increase the protein by 5 grams per serving, add 3 tablespoons of hulled hemp seeds.

Berries and Cream

Chard is a dark, leafy green that you may not see often in smoothie recipes. It is found in many different varieties and features crinkly green leaves with beautiful stalks ranging in color from red to pink to yellow. When enjoyed fresh, its taste resembles spinach, making it a great mild green to use for smoothies.

1 cup frozen mixed berries

1 cup chopped chard

2 tablespoons chia seeds

1 cup full-fat cottage cheese

1½ cups unsweetened almond milk

1. Put the berries, chard, chia seeds, cottage cheese, and almond milk in a blender. Blend on high speed until smooth.

2. Divide evenly between 2 cups and enjoy!

Per serving: Calories: 257; Total Fat: 12.9g; Sugars: 7.3g; Carbohydrates: 20.4g; Fiber: 10.5g; Protein: 17g; Sodium: 572mg

MAKES 2 (16-ounce) servings

PREP TIME 5 minutes

HEALTH HACK Don't discard the stalks from the chard; simply toss them in your blender with the leaves!

Protein-Powered Refuel

Cherry-Vanilla Revive

Cherries were one of my favorite fruits while I was growing up. I remember sitting at the table with my mom, chatting while we pitted cherries. It took twice as long to prepare them as it did to devour them, but I never minded. Now, I use cherries in post-workout smoothies like this one because of their ability to boost exercise performance and recovery.

1 cup frozen pitted cherries

1 banana, halved and frozen

½ cup chopped cucumber

3 tablespoons hulled hemp seeds

2 scoops vanilla protein powder

1½ cups water

MAKES 2 (14-ounce) servings

PREP TIME 5 minutes

SUBSTITUTE For a source of electrolytes and some natural sweetness, use coconut water as the liquid.

1. Put the cherries, banana, cucumber, hemp seeds, protein powder, and water in a blender. Blend on high speed until smooth.

2. Divide evenly between 2 cups and enjoy!

Per serving: Calories: 237; Total Fat: 8.6g; Sugars: 14.6g; Carbohydrates: 24g; Fiber: 2.9g; Protein: 19g; Sodium: 24.4mg

Blueberry-Oat

Dandelion greens are used in this recipe for their nutrient density. Their bitter taste is covered by the peanut butter and milk, but if you want a milder flavor to start, try swapping them with spinach. Try this recipe as a smoothie bowl topped with sliced bananas, chopped nuts, and a couple fresh blueberries.

1 cup frozen blueberries

1 cup chopped dandelion greens

½ cup rolled oats

3 tablespoons peanut butter

1½ cups whole milk

MAKES 2 (14-ounce) servings

PREP TIME 5 minutes

1. Put the blueberries, dandelion greens, oats, peanut butter, and milk in a blender. Blend on high speed until smooth.

2. Divide evenly between 2 cups and enjoy!

SUBSTITUTE For a dairy-free option, replace the milk with any plant-based milk or coconut water.

Per serving: Calories: 446; Total Fat: 20.9g; Sugars. 17.8g; Carbohydrates: 51.4g; Fiber: 8.6g; Protein: 19.1g; Sodium: 93.7mg

Protein-Powered Refuel

PB&J

Who doesn't love PB&J? Peanut butter and jelly come together for this spin on the classic childhood sandwich. Here, we're combining grapes and mixed berries for the "jelly" and using Greek yogurt for a smooth consistency. Feel free to play around with the fruit to test out different "jelly" flavors!

½ cup frozen red grapes

½ cup frozen mixed berries

1 cup fresh spinach

4 tablespoons peanut butter

1 cup full-fat plain Greek yogurt

½ cup water

MAKES 2 (16-ounce) servings

PREP TIME 5 minutes

1. Put the grapes, berries, spinach, peanut butter, yogurt, and water in a blender. Blend on high speed until smooth.

2. Divide evenly between 2 cups and enjoy!

Per serving: Calories: 342; Total Fat: 22.5g; Sugars: 11.3g; Carbohydrates: 18.1g; Fiber: 3.7g; Protein: 19.1g; Sodium: 90.5mg

SUBSTITUTE To make this peanut-free, simply swap the peanut butter for any nut butter. Just look for one without added sugars or hydrogenated oils.

Orangeade

While I'm a huge fan of some freshly squeezed orange juice, I don't enjoy the hit to my blood sugar. Instead, I've put together a winning combination of orange-pigmented fruits and vegetables to create an orange slushie I can enjoy in the morning without the midmorning crash.

2 medium oranges, peeled

½ cup frozen mango chunks

½ cup chopped golden beets

2 scoops protein powder

1½ cups coconut water

1. Put the oranges, mango, beets, protein powder, and coconut water in a blender. Blend on high speed until smooth.

2. Divide evenly between 2 cups and enjoy!

Per serving: Calories: 204; Total Fat: 1.7g; Sugars: 25g; Carbohydrates: 34.2g; Fiber: 6.5g; Protein: 15.8g; Sodium: 240mg

MAKES 2 (14-ounce) servings

PREP TIME 5 minutes

SUBSTITUTE Substitute orange fruits or vegetables, such as papaya, apricots, mangos, carrots, or sweet potatoes, for the oranges, mango, and beets in this smoothie.

Blackberry-Coconut-Fig

Figs are a sweet fruit that come from one of the world's oldest trees. These soft and chewy morsels are ripe when their skins are wrinkled, but their flesh is plump and tender. Since they are very delicate, they are often dried to preserve them so they are available throughout the year.

1 cup frozen blackberries

6 ripe figs, chopped

1 cup fresh spinach

2 scoops protein powder

1 cup coconut milk

½ cup water

1. Put the blackberries, figs, spinach, protein powder, coconut milk, and water in a blender. Blend on high speed until smooth.

2. Divide evenly between 2 cups and enjoy!

Per serving: Calories: 317; Total Fat: 13.9g; Sugars: 27.9g; Carbohydrates: 38.4g; Fiber: 8.2g; Protein: 16.2g; Sodium: 68.5mg

MAKES 2 (14-ounce) servings

PREP TIME 5 minutes

SUBSTITUTE If you can't find fresh figs, substitute dried figs or a fresh apricot or pear.

Cranberry-Orange Kefir

Collagen is one of the most abundant proteins in the body and has been shown to support joint health; improve the appearance of hair, skin, and nails; and decrease gut permeability. Collagen powder offers roughly 10 grams of protein per tablespoon.

1 medium orange, peeled
½ cup frozen cranberries
½ cup chopped carrots
1 cup plain kefir

3 tablespoons collagen powder
1½ cups water

MAKES 2 (14-ounce) servings
PREP TIME 5 minutes

1. Put the orange, cranberries, carrots, kefir, collagen powder, and water in a blender. Blend on high speed until smooth.

2. Divide evenly between 2 cups and enjoy!

SUBSTITUTE If you are unable to find collagen powder, replace it with another protein powder or with 3 tablespoons of hulled hemp seeds.

Per serving: Calories: 183; Total Fat: 4.2g; Sugars: 14.3g; Carbohydrates: 20.2g; Fiber: 3.5g; Protein: 18.4g; Sodium: 163mg

Fruity Bone Broth Refresher

Bone broth is made by simmering animal bones and tissues for long periods of time, often more than 24 hours. This mineral-rich broth is known for its benefits to the immune system and its ability to promote joint, digestive, and gut health. Although bone broth is flavorful, the fruit in this recipe takes center stage, so you won't even taste the broth!

1 cup frozen strawberries

1 banana, halved and frozen

1 cup chopped kale

1 cup full-fat plain Greek yogurt

1 cup bone broth

½ cup water

1. Put the strawberries, banana, kale, yogurt, bone broth, and water in a blender. Blend on high speed until smooth.

2. Divide evenly between 2 cups and enjoy!

Per serving: Calories: 220; Total Fat: 6.7g; Sugars: 10.9g; Carbohydrates: 22.7g; Fiber: 3.2g; Protein: 17.3g; Sodium: 228mg

MAKES 2 (16-ounce) servings

PREP TIME 5 minutes

SIMPLIFY Freeze bone broth in ice cube trays for quick additions to your smoothies or other recipes.

Key Lime

This recipe is basically protein-packed, guiltless key lime pie! Whenever I drink this smoothie, I picture myself in the Florida Keys. Cashews are used for their slightly sweet taste and protein content; however, cottage cheese can be used as a replacement. Add a tropical touch to this smoothie with some lime zest and vanilla.

2 bananas, halved and frozen

1 lime, peeled

⅓ cup raw cashews

2 scoops protein powder

½ cup coconut milk

1 cup water

MAKES 2 (12-ounce) servings

PREP TIME 5 minutes

SUPERCHARGE To incorporate a vegetable and add some green color to this smoothie, add a handful of spinach.

1. Put the bananas, lime, cashews, protein powder, coconut milk, and water in a blender. Blend on high speed until smooth.

2. Divide evenly between 2 cups and enjoy!

Per serving: Calories: 418; Total Fat: 23.9g; Sugars: 16.4g; Carbohydrates: 39.9g; Fiber: 4.8g; Protein: 19.5g; Sodium: 34.6mg

Magnesium Mint-Chocolate Chip

Sore muscles? Lactic acid buildup from exercise, as well as magnesium and potassium deficiencies, can sometimes be the culprits. In this recipe, chia seeds and cacao, both rich in magnesium, and bananas, which are a great source of potassium, can help relax fatigued and sore muscles.

2 tablespoons raw cacao powder

2 tablespoons chopped fresh mint leaves

2 bananas, halved and frozen

2 tablespoons chia seeds

1 cup full-fat plain Greek yogurt

1½ cups water

MAKES 2 (14-ounce) servings

PREP TIME 5 minutes

KID FRIENDLY For an extra-special garnish, top this smoothie with some whipped cream and cacao nibs.

1. Put the cacao powder, mint, bananas, chia seeds, yogurt, and water in a blender. Blend on high speed until smooth.

2. Divide evenly between 2 cups and enjoy!

Per serving: Calories: 310; Total Fat: 12.5g; Sugars: 14.5g; Carbohydrates: 37.9g; Fiber: 11.5g; Protein: 15.1g; Sodium: 53.6mg

Toasted Coconut and Papaya

Taking a little extra time to toast the coconut shreds makes this smoothie a little luxurious. We're using papaya for the tropical feel, but you can substitute mixed berries, pineapple, mango, or bananas. If this smoothie has a little too much coconut for your taste, try substituting coconut water for the coconut milk.

¼ cup unsweetened shredded coconut

1 cup frozen papaya chunks

1 cup chopped zucchini

2 scoops vanilla protein powder

1 cup coconut milk

½ cup water

1. Preheat the oven to 350°F.
2. Spread the shredded coconut on a baking sheet and bake in the oven for 3 to 6 minutes, or until lightly toasted. Let it cool to room temperature.
3. Put the toasted coconut, papaya, zucchini, protein powder, coconut milk, and water in a blender. Blend on high speed until smooth.
4. Divide evenly between 2 cups and enjoy!

Per serving: Calories: 378; Total Fat: 29.4g; Sugars: 10.2g; Carbohydrates: 17.7g; Fiber: 2.5g; Protein: 16.3g; Sodium: 75.9mg

MAKES 2 (16-ounce) servings

PREP TIME 10 minutes

SUPERCHARGE Add 2 tablespoons of flaxseed for some heart-healthy omega-3s.

CHAPTER 4

MAKE IT A MEAL

Green Monster

This high-calorie green smoothie will leave you full and satisfied from its fiber and healthy fats. The addition of leafy greens and the natural sweetness from the grapes makes for a well-rounded meal replacement.

2 cups chopped kale

1 avocado, peeled
  and pitted

1 cup frozen grapes

3 tablespoons hulled
  hemp seeds

1 cup coconut milk

½ cup water

1. Put the kale, avocado, grapes, hemp seeds, coconut milk, and water in a blender. Blend on high speed until smooth.

2. Divide evenly between 2 cups and enjoy!

Per serving: Calories: 554; Total Fat: 46.4g; Sugars: 12.3g; Carbohydrates: 33.1g; Fiber: 8.8g; Protein: 12g; Sodium: 52.1mg

MAKES 2 (14-ounce) servings

PREP TIME 5 minutes

KID FRIENDLY If you are easing into green smoothies, swap milder spinach for the kale.

Orange Sunrise

Confused by all the varieties of oats? The difference between steel-cut, rolled, and quick oats lies in the degree to which the oats are processed, which affects their texture and health benefits. For smoothie-making, I recommend rolled oats, which are steamed, and then pressed flat with steel rollers. Once blended, they soften quickly and contribute to a smooth texture.

1 cup frozen mango chunks

½ cup rolled oats

1 cup full-fat plain Greek yogurt

2 tablespoons cashew butter

2 cups unsweetened almond milk

MAKES 2 (16-ounce) servings

PREP TIME 5 minutes

1. Put the mango, oats, yogurt, cashew butter, and almond milk in a blender. Blend on high speed until smooth.

2. Divide evenly between 2 cups and enjoy!

SUBSTITUTE For an oat substitute, try using cooked quinoa. This pseudo-cereal grain is a complete protein and a great source of fiber, magnesium, and iron.

Per serving: Calories: 441; Total Fat: 19.8g; Sugars: 12.2g; Carbohydrates: 45.3g; Fiber: 6.9g; Protein: 20.8g; Sodium: 212mg

Make It a Meal

Purple Passion

Purple fruits and vegetables are known for a powerful antioxidant, anthocyanin. This plant pigment gives them their deep red, purple, or blue hues and is known for improving heart health, boosting cognitive function, and preventing cancer.

2 plums, diced and frozen

1 cup frozen blackberries

1 avocado, peeled and pitted

1½ cups full-fat cottage cheese

1½ cups unsweetened almond milk

MAKES 2 (16-ounce) servings

PREP TIME 5 minutes

1. Put the plums, blackberries, avocado, cottage cheese, and almond milk in a blender. Blend on high speed until smooth.
2. Divide evenly between 2 cups and enjoy!

SUPERCHARGE Add in a purple vegetable such as shredded red cabbage, purple sweet potato, raw eggplant, purple carrots, or purple cauliflower.

Per serving: Calories: 414; Total Fat: 24.8g; Sugars: 15.2g; Carbohydrates: 29.9g; Fiber: 12.2g; Protein: 23g; Sodium: 742mg

Banana-Nut-Oat

Start your day with a healthy banana muffin alternative that contains a balance of nutrients to leave you feeling full and energized for the day. The walnuts and coconut oil in this recipe balance out the carbohydrates from the oats. Add a tablespoon of nut butter, a dash of cinnamon, or even some cacao powder for more variety!

2 bananas, halved and frozen

½ cup walnuts

½ cup rolled oats

1 tablespoon coconut oil

1½ cups unsweetened almond milk

1. Put the bananas, walnuts, oats, coconut oil, and almond milk in a blender. Blend on high speed until smooth.

2. Divide evenly between 2 cups and enjoy!

Per serving: Calories: 532; Total Fat: 31.2g; Sugars: 15.2g; Carbohydrates: 57.6g; Fiber: 9.9g; Protein: 13.1g; Sodium: 123mg

MAKES 2 (14-ounce) servings

PREP TIME 5 minutes

HEALTH HACK Add 2 scoops of protein powder to double the protein in this smoothie.

Make It a Meal

Blueberry Lemonade

As a kid, I would routinely set up lemonade stands in my front yard with my friends. This smoothie delivers a classic lemonade slushie with a blueberry twist. If only I had come up with this fun creation when I was a child; I would be a millionaire! For a playful pink lemonade variation, use strawberries, cherries, or raspberries instead of the blueberries. Garnish it with some fresh berries and a lemon slice.

2 cups frozen blueberries

1 lemon, peeled

1 avocado, peeled and pitted

1½ cups full-fat plain yogurt

2 scoops protein powder

¾ cup water

MAKES 2 (16-ounce) servings

PREP TIME 5 minutes

1. Put the blueberries, lemon, avocado, yogurt, protein powder, and water in a blender. Blend on high speed until smooth.

2. Divide evenly between 2 cups and enjoy!

Per serving: Calories: 424; Total Fat: 22.8g; Sugars: 23.4g; Carbohydrates: 39.9g; Fiber: 12.1g; Protein: 22g; Sodium: 116mg

SIMPLIFY Lemons, limes, grapefruit, and oranges can be frozen. Peel and chop them, then pop them in the freezer for even easier smoothies. They also make flavorful ice cubes to add to your glass of water!

Red Lava

Hemp seeds are little nuggets of nutrition rich in magnesium, zinc, omegas, fiber, and other micronutrients. They also offer a great source of plant-based protein, packing 10 grams into just three tablespoons. You can find hemp seeds online or at most grocery stores. Just make sure to buy hulled hemp hearts and not the ones in the shell.

1 cup chopped red beets

1½ cups frozen strawberries

3 tablespoons hulled
  hemp seeds

1 avocado, peeled and pitted

1 cup coconut milk

1 cup water

1. Put the beets, strawberries, hemp seeds, avocado, coconut milk, and water in a blender. Blend on high speed until smooth.

2. Divide evenly between 2 cups and enjoy!

Per serving: Calories: 534; Total Fat: 46.3g; Sugars: 10.8g; Carbohydrates: 28g; Fiber: 10.9g; Protein: 11.2g; Sodium: 75.9mg

MAKES 2 (16-ounce) servings

PREP TIME 5 minutes

SUPERCHARGE Add a bit of heat to the lava with a dash of cayenne pepper. Cayenne has been shown to support healthy digestion, reduce pain, lower cholesterol, and improve circulation.

Mr. Golden Sun

My son and I sometimes play a game where he'll tell me what color smoothie he wants, and I'll try to create it. I give myself bonus points when I can sneak a hidden vegetable in. This orange smoothie has hidden golden beets, which are a variety of beet that lacks the vibrant red pigment. They tend to be milder and sweeter than red beets, so they can be an easier vegetable to hide. Their color has me singing the "Mr. Golden Sun" song every time I make it.

1 nectarine, diced and frozen

1 orange, peeled

1 cup diced golden beets, frozen

1 cup full-fat plain yogurt

1½ cups coconut milk

MAKES 2 (16-ounce) servings

PREP TIME 5 minutes

HEALTH HACK Boost the protein by 10 grams per serving by adding 3 tablespoons of hulled hemp seeds.

1. Put the nectarine, orange, beets, yogurt, and coconut milk in a blender. Blend on high speed until smooth.

2. Divide evenly between 2 cups and enjoy!

Per serving: Calories: 504; Total Fat: 40.6g; Sugars: 21.9g; Carbohydrates: 33.3g; Fiber: 4.7g; Protein: 10.2g; Sodium: 132mg

Spiced Pear Overnight Oats Smoothie

Don't let the name fool you; overnight oats take only a couple minutes of prep. Mix them up the night before, then just give them a quick whirl in the blender the next morning! Soaking the oats overnight improves their digestibility and supplies a source of resistant starch, which increases the feeling of fullness, improves insulin sensitivity, and feeds the good gut bacteria.

1 cup rolled oats

1½ cups unsweetened almond milk, divided

2 pears, diced and frozen

1 banana, halved and frozen

¼ teaspoon ground nutmeg

MAKES 2 (14-ounce) servings

PREP TIME 5 minutes, plus overnight to chill

1. The night before, add the oats and 1 cup of the almond milk to a blender jar. With a spoon or spatula, give it a quick stir to combine. Cover the blender jar and put it in the refrigerator overnight, or for at least 3 hours.

2. When you're ready to make the smoothie, put the pears, banana, nutmeg, and remaining ½ cup of almond milk in the blender. Blend on high speed until smooth, adding more milk if necessary.

3. Divide evenly between 2 cups and enjoy!

SIMPLIFY Forget to prepare this the night before? No problem. You can still make this recipe for an on-the-go smoothie. Just add all the ingredients to the blender and blend on high. The smoothie may not be quite as smooth, but it will still be delicious and nutritious!

Per serving: Calories: 433; Total Fat: 8.1g; Sugars: 15.8g; Carbohydrates: 78.9g; Fiber: 14.9g; Protein: 15.2g; Sodium: 122mg

Make It a Meal

Piña Colada

If you like piña coladas and getting caught in the rain, then this smoothie is for you. When purchasing any type of nuts, look for those that are organic and raw. Soaking and sprouting them before you use them can increase the digestibility of the nutrients. Whenever you are using nuts in a smoothie, be sure to let your blender whirl for an extra 30 to 60 seconds to make sure they are properly incorporated into the smoothie for a smooth texture.

**1½ cups frozen
   pineapple chunks**
1 lime, peeled
½ cup raw cashews
1 avocado, peeled and pitted
1½ cups coconut milk yogurt
1 cup water

1. Put the pineapple, lime, cashews, avocado, yogurt, and water in a blender. Blend on high speed until smooth.

2. Divide evenly between 2 cups and enjoy!

Per serving: Calories: 514; Total Fat: 34.4g; Sugars: 14.8g; Carbohydrates: 48.1g; Fiber: 10.2g; Protein: 8.7g; Sodium: 11.8mg

MAKES 2 (16-ounce) servings
PREP TIME 5 minutes

HEALTH HACK If you're looking for more protein, swap the coconut milk yogurt with Greek yogurt. This will increase the protein by 13.5 grams per serving, but you will lose the coconut flavor.

Berry Brain Booster

When I find that my brainpower is lagging from a busy schedule from kids, housework, and work, I put this smoothie on my to-make list. Walnuts and flax-seed both contain omega-3 fatty acids, which improve memory and focus, while antioxidant-rich blueberries support cognitive function and protect against memory loss.

1½ cups frozen blueberries
1 banana, halved and frozen
¼ cup walnuts

2 tablespoons ground flaxseed
1 cup coconut milk
½ cup water

MAKES 2 (16-ounce) servings
PREP TIME 5 minutes

1. Put the blueberries, banana, walnuts, flaxseed, coconut milk, and water in a blender. Blend on high speed until smooth.

2. Divide evenly between 2 cups and enjoy!

HEALTH HACK Add 2 tablespoons of collagen powder to boost the protein by 10 grams per serving.

Per serving: Calories: 467; Total Fat: 37.5g; Sugars: 17.5g; Carbohydrates: 34.8g; Fiber: 7.6g; Protein: 6.9g; Sodium: 18.8mg

Make It a Meal

Rise and Shine

Time to rise and shine! Eating oatmeal by itself for breakfast runs the risk of spiking your blood sugar and leaving you feeling hungry quickly. This smoothie will start your day off right with healthy fat and protein to balance the carbohydrates from the oats. No sugar crashes here!

½ **cup diced**
   cantaloupe, frozen
1 cup frozen blackberries
1 cup rolled oats

1 avocado, peeled and pitted
2 cups unsweetened
   almond milk

MAKES 2 (16-ounce) servings
PREP TIME 5 minutes

HEALTH HACK Boost the protein by 15 grams per serving by adding one cup of cottage cheese.

1. Put the cantaloupe, blackberries, oats, avocado, and almond milk in a blender. Blend on high speed until smooth.

2. Divide evenly between 2 cups and enjoy!

Per serving: Calories: 544; Total Fat: 23.5g; Sugars: 7.3g; Carbohydrates: 72.1g; Fiber: 20.2g; Protein: 17.5g; Sodium: 176mg

Superfood Supreme

"Superfood" has become quite the buzzword in recent years. It sounds intimidating, but it simply refers to foods that pack a big punch of nutrition, like açai and spirulina. Fortunately, plenty of familiar foods can also claim this superstar status. Cherries and other berries qualify with their potent vitamins, antioxidants, and phytochemicals, while chia seeds and avocados nourish with heart-healthy omega-3s, magnesium, vitamin E, and fiber. This smoothie blends all four for the ultimate superfood energy boost!

1 cup frozen pitted cherries

1½ cups frozen mixed berries

1 avocado, peeled and pitted

2 tablespoons chia seeds

2 cups full-fat plain yogurt

½ cup water

MAKES 2 (16-ounce) servings

PREP TIME 5 minutes

1. Put the cherries, berries, avocado, chia seeds, yogurt, and water in a blender. Blend on high speed until smooth.

2. Divide evenly between 2 cups and enjoy!

SUPERCHARGE Supercharge this smoothie by adding another superfood, such as chard, kale, or any other dark, leafy green.

Per serving: Calories: 427; Total Fat: 25g; Sugars: 24.5g; Carbohydrates: 42.8g; Fiber: 15.1g; Protein: 14.2g; Sodium: 123mg

Make It a Meal

Cardamom-Chia Smoothie Bowl

Want to kick your smoothie up a notch? Grab your spoon and try a smoothie bowl! This simple switch can transform your smoothie from a quick gulp to a more lavish experience. The best part about smoothie bowls is that you can add garnishes to glam them up. I recommend topping this one with chopped pecans, a dash of Ceylon cinnamon, and coconut flakes. I prefer Ceylon cinnamon, which is "true" cinnamon. Cassia cinnamon has been found to contain a compound called coumarin, which may be harmful in large doses.

2 pears, diced and frozen
2 tablespoons chia seeds
½ teaspoon ground cardamom

2 tablespoons almond butter
1 cup coconut milk
½ cup water

MAKES 2 (12-ounce) servings
PREP TIME 5 minutes

1. Put the pears, chia seeds, cardamom, almond butter, coconut milk, and water in a blender. Blend on high speed until smooth.
2. Divide evenly between 2 bowls and enjoy!

SUPERCHARGE Sneak a serving of vegetables into this smoothie by adding chopped cauliflower.

Per serving: Calories: 461; Total Fat: 39.2g; Sugars: 8.6g; Carbohydrates: 27.2g; Fiber: 11.6g; Protein: 8g; Sodium: 19.8mg

Orange Twist & Shout

Flaxseeds are one of the richest sources of alpha-linolenic acid (ALA), a type of omega-3 fatty acid. These anti-inflammatory fats are known for improving circulation and heart health. Flaxseeds are also a great source of lignans, a plant compound known for its antioxidant activity, which promotes blood sugar and hormone balance. Be aware that the body is unable to digest whole flaxseed, so purchase them ground or grind them yourself before using them.

2 oranges, peeled

1 banana, halved
   and frozen

½ cup rolled oats

2 tablespoons ground
   flaxseed

1 cup coconut milk yogurt

1 cup water

1. Put the oranges, banana, oats, flaxseed, yogurt, and water in a blender. Blend on high speed until smooth.

2. Divide evenly between 2 cups and enjoy!

Per serving: Calories: 410; Total Fat: 12g; Sugars: 19.2g; Carbohydrates: 66.9g; Fiber: 10.7g; Protein: 10.8g; Sodium: 4.9mg

MAKES 2 (16-ounce) servings

PREP TIME 5 minutes

HEALTH HACK Balance this smoothie with more healthy fat by adding a tablespoon of coconut oil.

Pomegranate-Raspberry

Coconut milk is loaded with nutrients, such as fiber, manganese, iron, and magnesium. This popular dairy alternative also contains lauric acid, which is a protective fatty acid that may help reduce cholesterol levels. When shopping for coconut milk, look for one that is simply coconut and water, without any added sugars, additives, or flavor enhancers.

1 cup frozen raspberries

1 cup pomegranate seeds

1 cup full-fat plain yogurt

¼ cup sunflower seeds

1 cup coconut milk

½ cup water

1. Put the raspberries, pomegranate seeds, yogurt, sunflower seeds, coconut milk, and water in a blender. Blend on high speed until smooth.

2. Divide evenly between 2 cups and enjoy!

Per serving: Calories: 504; Total Fat: 38.5g; Sugars:20.8g; Carbohydrates: 36g; Fiber: 9g; Protein: 12.4g; Sodium: 75.8mg

MAKES 2 (16-ounce) servings

PREP TIME 5 minutes

SUBSTITUTE If you are unable to find pomegranate seeds, use a quarter cup of pomegranate juice instead.

Probiotic Coco-Loco

The subtle, sweet taste of coconut brings the tropics right to your doorstep. We're using banana as the fruit in this recipe, but you can use any tropical fruit you'd like, such as pineapple, mango, papaya, or guava. Adding a little lime juice, lime zest, and vanilla would further spruce up this smoothie for a refreshing treat.

2 bananas, halved and frozen

¼ cup shredded coconut

1 cup coconut milk yogurt

½ cup rolled oats

2 tablespoons chia seeds

1½ cups water

MAKES 2 (14-ounce) servings

PREP TIME 5 minutes

SUPERCHARGE Make a chocolate version of this smoothie by adding 2 tablespoons of cacao powder.

1. Put the bananas, coconut, yogurt, oats, chia seeds, and water in a blender. Blend on high speed until smooth.

2. Divide evenly between 2 cups and enjoy!

Per serving: Calories: 501; Total Fat: 18.6g; Sugars: 19.5g; Carbohydrates: 74g; Fiber: 14.3g; Protein: 11.9g; Sodium: 35.7mg

Morning Melon

When cantaloupe is at its ripest, it is sweet and juicy and a perfect addition to smoothies. You'll know your melon is ripe when it is firm but not too hard. When you gently press on the blossom end, you should feel a bit of give, and it should smell lightly sweet. This delectable summer melon is also high in vitamin C, beta-carotene, folate, magnesium, and antioxidants.

½ cup diced cantaloupe

½ cup frozen sliced peaches

1 cup rolled oats

1 cup full-fat plain Greek yogurt

1½ cups unsweetened almond milk

1. Put the cantaloupe, peaches, oats, yogurt, and almond milk in a blender. Blend on high speed until smooth.

2. Divide evenly between 2 cups and enjoy!

Per serving: Calories: 466; Total Fat: 13.8g; Sugars: 6.7g; Carbohydrates: 60.1g; Fiber: 10g; Protein: 24.6g; Sodium: 176mg

MAKES 2 (16-ounce) servings

PREP TIME 5 minutes

SUPERCHARGE Add a one-inch piece of ginger, sliced, to the smoothie for extra flavor. Ginger has natural anti-inflammatory properties and helps stimulate the digestive system.

The Glow Up

Eat your way to a glowing complexion with this skin-loving smoothie! Vitamin C—found in the pineapple, orange, and bell pepper in this recipe—is important for collagen formation and fighting free radicals, which damage our skin cells. Avocados and walnuts are both great sources of vitamin E, which protects skin from oxidative damage and supports skin growth.

1 cup frozen
   pineapple chunks

1 orange, peeled

1 red bell pepper, chopped

1 avocado, diced and frozen

½ cup walnuts

1½ cups water

MAKES 2 (14-ounce) servings

PREP TIME 5 minutes

1. Put the pineapple, orange, bell pepper, avocado, walnuts, and water in a blender. Blend on high speed until smooth.

2. Divide evenly between 2 cups and enjoy!

SUPERCHARGE Toss in a handful of pumpkin seeds for extra zinc, which helps skin heal.

Per serving: Calories: 451; Total Fat: 34.2g; Sugars: 18.6g; Carbohydrates: 36.9g; Fiber: 13g; Protein: 8.3g; Sodium: 12.1mg

Make It a Meal

Cherry-Almond-Chia

Don't be afraid to use brown bananas! The browner your banana, the higher its sugar content, so adding one to your smoothie will make it naturally sweet. On the other hand, green-tipped bananas offer a great source of resistant starch, which feeds gut bacteria and helps balance blood sugar. Choose the one you need!

1½ cups frozen pitted cherries

¼ cup almonds

3 tablespoons chia seeds

2 bananas, halved and frozen

1½ cups plain kefir

½ cup water

MAKES 2 (16-ounce) servings

PREP TIME 5 minutes

HEALTH HACK Make this smoothie dairy-free by using a kefir made from almond milk or coconut milk.

1. Put the cherries, almonds, chia seeds, bananas, kefir, and water in a blender. Blend on high speed until smooth.

2. Divide evenly between 2 cups and enjoy!

Per serving: Calories: 477; Total Fat: 22.5g; Sugars: 34.8g; Carbohydrates: 61.3g; Fiber: 14.9g; Protein: 15.4g; Sodium: 96.5mg

Apple-Cinnamon-Raisin

In ancient Rome, cinnamon was considered more precious than gold. The most well-known benefits of cinnamon are its abilities to stabilize blood sugar, relieve digestive discomfort, and act as an antimicrobial. In smoothies, this warming spice brings sweetness without any added sugar. Garnish this smoothie with a dash of cinnamon and a sprinkle of raisins on top for a pretty presentation.

1 red apple, chopped and frozen

1 teaspoon ground cinnamon

½ cup seedless raisins

1 cup rolled oats

2 cups whole milk

MAKES 2 (14-ounce) servings

PREP TIME 5 minutes

1. Put the apple, cinnamon, raisins, oats, and milk in a blender. Blend on high speed until smooth.
2. Divide evenly between 2 cups and enjoy!

HEALTH HACK Boost the protein and fat contents by adding a spoonful or two of nut butter.

Per serving: Calories: 547; Total Fat: 13.5g; Sugars: 31.6g; Carbohydrates: 90.5g; Fiber: 11.2g; Protein: 21.8g; Sodium: 102mg

Make It a Meal

Strawberry-Coconut

Both shredded coconut and coconut milk are used in this recipe to bring out that sweet, rich coconut flavor. If that's too much coconut for you, mellow it by replacing the coconut milk with coconut water, cow's milk, or another plant-based milk. If needed, toasted coconut chips, often found in the snack aisles of grocery stores, can be a great replacement for shredded coconut.

1½ cups frozen strawberries

2 tablespoons chia seeds

2 bananas, halved
    and frozen

¼ cup unsweetened
    shredded coconut

1 cup coconut milk

½ cup water

MAKES 2 (14-ounce) servings

PREP TIME 5 minutes

HEALTH HACK Reduce the carb content of this smoothie by 36 grams by substituting an avocado for the bananas.

1. Put the strawberries, chia seeds, bananas, shredded coconut, coconut milk, and water in a blender. Blend on high speed until smooth.

2. Divide evenly between 2 cups and enjoy!

Per serving: Calories: 530; Total Fat: 34.2g; Sugars: 27g; Carbohydrates: 58.5g; Fiber: 13.7g; Protein: 7.3g; Sodium: 53mg

Mango Tango

When I'm struggling to get my kids to eat anything green, this is my go-to smoothie. The mango in this recipe easily masks any sign of spinach, but any bold-flavored fruit usually does the trick. Try replacing the mango with papaya, pineapple, or mixed berries for more variety.

1½ cups frozen mango chunks
1 cup fresh spinach
½ cup almonds
1 avocado, peeled and pitted
1½ cups unsweetened almond milk

1. Put the mango, spinach almonds, avocado, and almond milk in a blender. Blend on high speed until smooth.
2. Divide evenly between 2 cups and enjoy!

HEALTH HACK Boost the protein in this smoothie by adding a cup of Greek yogurt for an extra 12 grams per serving.

Per serving: Calories: 437; Total Fat: 31.9g; Sugars: 20.5g; Carbohydrates: 35.5g; Fiber: 12.1g; Protein: 10.9g; Sodium: 164mg

Make It a Meal

Blueberry-Pom

Pomegranate has long been coveted as a symbol of prosperity, hope, and abundance by many cultures and religions throughout the world. This ancient fruit is often incorporated into artwork or used as a ceremonial part of celebrations and religious gatherings. Whether you're looking for prosperity or to reap the numerous health benefits of pomegranates, you're sure to win with this smoothie.

1 cup frozen blueberries

1 cup pomegranate seeds

1½ cups full-fat plain Greek yogurt

2 tablespoons chia seeds

1 avocado, peeled and pitted

1½ cups water

1. Put the blueberries, pomegranate seeds, yogurt, chia seeds, avocado, and water in a blender. Blend on high speed until smooth.

2. Divide evenly between 2 cups and enjoy!

Per serving: Calories: 518; Total Fat: 30.6g; Sugars: 19.1g; Carbohydrates: 41.9g; Fiber: 18.9g; Protein: 21.5g; Sodium: 85mg

MAKES 2 (16-ounce) servings

PREP TIME 5 minutes

SUPERCHARGE Add a serving of vegetables by adding one cup of leafy greens such as spinach, kale, or chard to this smoothie.

Spiced Pumpkin Pecan

Pumpkin spice, hayrides, and the cool and crisp air are my favorite parts of fall. Pumpkin is a rich source of the powerful antioxidant beta-carotene and offers folate and magnesium. Plus, the comforting combination of pecans, cinnamon, and pumpkin will bring fall right into your cup!

1 cup pumpkin puree
1 banana, halved and frozen
½ teaspoon ground cinnamon

¼ cup pecans
1½ cups coconut milk

MAKES 2 (14-ounce) servings
PREP TIME 5 minutes

1. Put the pumpkin, banana, cinnamon, pecans, and coconut milk in a blender. Blend on high speed until smooth.

2. Divide evenly between 2 cups and enjoy!

SUPERCHARGE Add other health-promoting spices, such as ginger, nutmeg, and ground cloves, to up the flavor and antioxidants.

Per serving: Calories: 524; Total Fat: 46.5g; Sugars: 11.8g; Carbohydrates: 30.6g; Fiber: 6.7g; Protein: 6.7g; Sodium: 28.8mg

Apple-Parsnip

Parsnips bring a wide variety of nutrients to this smoothie, including folate, fiber, potassium, and vitamin C. This cream-colored root vegetable resembles carrots in shape and taste and can be eaten both raw and cooked. Smoothies aside, I also love eating this vegetable mashed or as roasted fries.

1 red apple, diced
½ cup diced parsnip
½ cup rolled oats

½ cup walnuts
2 cups whole milk

MAKES 2 (14-ounce) servings
PREP TIME 5 minutes

1. Put the apple, parsnip, oats, walnuts, and milk in a blender. Blend on high speed until smooth.
2. Divide evenly between 2 cups and enjoy!

SUBSTITUTE If you're unable to find parsnips, replace them with carrots.

Per serving: Calories: 442; Total Fat: 23g; Sugars: 11.9g; Carbohydrates: 51.9g; Fiber: 10.9g; Protein: 12.9g; Sodium: 19.8mg

Berry-Chocolate

Did you know that cocoa is from fermented cacao seeds? The seeds are processed at high temperatures to yield cocoa's signature sweetness. Cacao, on the other hand, is processed at low temperatures, thereby retaining its nutritional benefits. Raw cacao powder provides an excellent source of calcium, iron, magnesium, and antioxidants, so go ahead and get your chocolate fix!

1½ cups frozen
  mixed berries
½ tablespoon raw
  cacao powder

1 avocado, peeled and pitted
1 cup full-fat plain
  Greek yogurt
2 cups whole milk

1. Put the berries, cacao powder, avocado, yogurt and milk in a blender. Blend on high speed until smooth.

2. Divide evenly between 2 cups and enjoy!

Per serving: Calories: 474; Total Fat: 29.3g; Sugars: 21g; Carbohydrates: 36.2g; Fiber: 11.8g; Protein: 21g; Sodium: 154mg

MAKES 2 (12-ounce) servings
PREP TIME 5 minutes

SIMPLIFY Keep chopped avocados in the freezer for faster smoothies. To prevent them from sticking together, dice them and spread them evenly across a baking sheet lined with parchment paper. Freeze the diced avocado, then transfer it to a storage container once solid.

Make It a Meal

The Pink Smoothie

This recipe includes not one, but two hidden vegetables to give the smoothie its dreamy pink color. If you need to sweeten this up a bit to mask the earthy taste from the beets, toss in some extra berries or a few pitted dates.

½ cup chopped red
   beets, frozen

1 cup frozen raspberries

½ cup chopped cauliflower

2 tablespoons
   collagen powder

2 cups coconut milk

1. Put the beets, raspberries, cauliflower, collagen powder, and coconut milk in a blender. Blend on high speed until smooth.

2. Divide evenly between 2 cups and enjoy!

Per serving: Calories: 533; Total Fat: 48.7g; Sugars: 5.6g; Carbohydrates: 18.3g; Fiber: 5.6g; Protein: 15.3g; Sodium: 119mg

MAKES 2 (16-ounce) servings

PREP TIME 5 minutes

SIMPLIFY Purchase ready-to-go frozen cauliflower rice in the freezer section at the grocery store to minimize prep and cleanup time.

Holiday in a Cup

Seasonal smoothies are my favorite because they add a natural variety to my diet. This smoothie brings the festive flavors of cranberry and pomegranate, reminiscent of a stroll through a winter wonderland. If you can't find cranberries, substitute with raspberries, a pear, or a red apple.

1 cup frozen cranberries

1 cup pomegranate seeds

1 avocado, peeled and pitted

3 tablespoons hulled hemp seeds

1½ cups coconut milk yogurt

1 cup water

MAKES 2 (16-ounce) servings

PREP TIME 5 minutes

1. Put the cranberries, pomegranate seeds, avocado, hemp seeds, yogurt, and water in a blender. Blend on high speed until smooth.

2. Divide evenly between 2 cups and enjoy!

Per serving: Calories: 493; Total Fat: 31.8g; Sugars: 14.8g; Carbohydrates: 44.6g; Fiber: 12.7g; Protein: 10.2g; Sodium: 10.7mg

SUPERCHARGE Add rosemary for an extra dash of holiday flavor. Rosemary is known for supporting hair growth, improving memory, and boosting the immune system.

Make It a Meal

Golden Milk

This is my smoothie rendition of golden milk, or haldi doodh, *which is a traditional beverage from India. It has been used in Ayurvedic medicine for thousands of years to address health concerns, such as digestive issues, joint pains, and fatigue. The health benefits come primarily from the spices, which offer antioxidant, anti-cancer, and antimicrobial properties.*

2 bananas, halved and frozen

½ cup full-fat cottage cheese

1 teaspoon ground turmeric

1 teaspoon ground cinnamon

2 cups coconut milk

MAKES 2 (12-ounce) servings

PREP TIME 5 minutes

1. Put the bananas, cottage cheese, turmeric, cinnamon, and coconut milk in a blender. Blend on high speed until smooth.

2. Divide evenly between 2 cups and enjoy!

SUPERCHARGE Experiment with incorporating some of the traditionally used spices, including ginger, cardamom, and black pepper.

Per serving: Calories: 612; Total Fat: 51g; Sugars: 15.9g; Carbohydrates: 37.7g; Fiber: 4.5g; Protein: 11.9g; Sodium: 223mg

Out of This Galaxy

Chia seeds are jam-packed with nutrition. Just one tablespoon of these little black seeds offers five grams of fiber and two grams of protein. They are also a great source of plant-based omega-3s. Unlike most seeds, chia seeds are very absorbent, creating a gel when they are in contact with moisture, which provides a unique texture to your smoothie!

1 cup frozen mixed berries

1 cup frozen pineapple chunks

1 avocado, peeled and pitted

2 tablespoons chia seeds

1 cup coconut milk

1 cup water

1. Put the berries, pineapple, avocado, chia seeds, coconut milk, and water in a blender. Blend on high speed until smooth.

2. Divide evenly between 2 cups and enjoy!

Per serving: Calories: 548; Total Fat: 45g; Sugars: 12.9g; Carbohydrates: 38.2g; Fiber: 17.8g; Protein: 8.3g; Sodium: 26.8mg

MAKES 2 (16-ounce) servings

PREP TIME 5 minutes

HEALTH HACK Toss in one cup of chopped zucchini for an extra serving of vegetables.

Make It a Meal

CHAPTER 5

GLASS FULL OF GREENS

Green Supreme

Collard greens may not be your first go-to green for smoothies, but these mighty greens contain impressive amounts of vitamins K, C, and A; manganese; and calcium. Part of the cruciferous vegetable family, collard greens have a light and slightly bitter taste, but you won't even notice it with the addition of pineapple and coconut water.

½ medium grapefruit, peeled

1 cup frozen
   pineapple chunks

2 cups chopped
   collard greens

1 (1-inch) piece ginger, sliced

1½ cups coconut water

MAKES 2 (14-ounce) servings

PREP TIME 5 minutes

HEALTH HACK Add more healthy fat to this smoothie with an avocado.

1. Put the grapefruit, pineapple, collard greens, ginger, and coconut water in a blender. Blend on high speed until smooth.

2. Divide evenly between 2 cups and enjoy!

Per serving: Calories: 113; Total Fat: 0.7g; Sugars: 17.6g; Carbohydrates: 26.4g; Fiber: 4.8g; Protein: 3g; Sodium: 267mg

Kale-Banana

If you're new to using kale in green smoothies, try this recipe first. The sweet banana and the smoothness from the coconut milk will make you forget that you're drinking your greens.

1 banana, halved
  and frozen
1 cup chopped cucumber
2 cups chopped kale

2 tablespoons ground
  flaxseed
1 cup coconut milk
½ cup water

1. Put the banana, cucumber, kale, flaxseed, coconut milk, and water in a blender. Blend on high speed until smooth.

2. Divide evenly between 2 cups and enjoy!

Per serving: Calories: 488; Total Fat: 38.7g; Sugars: 15.3g; Carbohydrates: 38.7g; Fiber: 4.7g; Protein: 6.1g; Sodium: 45.7mg

MAKES 2 (14-ounce) servings
PREP TIME 5 minutes

SUBSTITUTE Other greens, such as chard, dandelion greens, arugula, and micro-greens, work well in this smoothie.

Apple Tart

You may be surprised to see apple cider vinegar in a smoothie. However, it's known for reducing reflux symptoms, supporting blood sugar and gut health, and improving the appearance of the skin. A little bit of this fermented apple cider will add just the right amount of tang to your smoothie. Look for raw, unfiltered apple cider vinegar to ensure that it contains the gut-loving probiotics and enzymes.

1 red apple, chopped and frozen

2 cups chopped Boston lettuce

1 avocado, chopped and frozen

½ cup walnuts

1 tablespoon apple cider vinegar

1½ cups water

MAKES 2 (14-ounce) servings

PREP TIME 5 minutes

KID FRIENDLY If this smoothie is too tart for you, cut back on the apple cider vinegar or replace it with ½ cup plain yogurt for the probiotics.

1. Put the apple, lettuce, avocado, walnuts, vinegar, and water in a blender. Blend on high speed until smooth.

2. Divide evenly between 2 cups and enjoy!

Per serving: Calories: 407; Total Fat: 34.1g; Sugars: 11.4g; Carbohydrates: 26.4g; Fiber: 11.5g; Protein: 7.4g; Sodium: 11.3mg

Kiwi, Zucchini, and Pear

Why use just one vegetable when you can use more? Zucchini is my secret smoothie veggie. With a neutral taste, it boosts your smoothie with fiber, potassium, manganese, vitamin C, and vitamin A, while also adding some creaminess.

2 kiwis, peeled, chopped, and frozen

1 cup chopped zucchini

1 pear, chopped and frozen

1 cup fresh spinach

1½ cups unsweetened almond milk

MAKES 2 (16-ounce) servings

PREP TIME 5 minutes

1. Put the kiwi, zucchini, pear, spinach, and almond milk in a blender. Blend on high speed until smooth.

2. Divide evenly between 2 cups and enjoy!

SIMPLIFY Purchase spiralized zucchini to use in smoothies and as a pasta substitute. They can be found fresh or frozen at most grocery stores.

Per serving: Calories: 121; Total Fat: 3g; Sugars: 13.6g; Carbohydrates: 23.4g; Fiber: 6.4g; Protein: 3.3g; Sodium: 165mg

Green Mango

I simply used to dump my radish greens in the trash until I realized I was tossing away valuable nutrition! With their high levels of essential nutrients, such as vitamin C, folate, iron, and calcium, these peppery greens don't get the glory they deserve. Make sure to wash them well, as radish greens can trap a lot of grit. You can also try them sautéed or added to soups and salads.

1 cup frozen mango chunks

2 cups chopped
   radish greens

1 avocado, peeled and pitted

2 tablespoons chia seeds

1 cup full-fat plain
   Greek yogurt

1½ cups water

MAKES 2 (16-ounce) servings

PREP TIME 5 minutes

1. Put the mango, radish greens, avocado, chia seeds, yogurt, and water in a blender. Blend on high speed until smooth.

2. Divide evenly between 2 cups and enjoy!

Per serving: Calories: 440; Total Fat: 26.8g; Sugars: 12.9g; Carbohydrates: 37g; Fiber: 16.2g; Protein: 17.4g; Sodium: 88.3mg

SUPERCHARGE Ground cardamom adds a flavorful sweet and savory dynamic and has long been used for oral health, supporting digestion, and cancer protection. Add a teaspoon for extra zing and nutrition.

Ginger Crisp

Arugula is a member of the cruciferous family, along with broccoli, cauliflower, and cabbage. This leafy green contains similar cancer-fighting compounds as other cruciferous vegetables. In this smoothie, the unique, bright, peppery taste of the arugula teams up with the ginger and pear to provide a sweet, crisp taste.

2 pears, chopped and frozen

2 cups arugula

1 avocado, peeled
 and pitted

1 (1-inch) piece ginger, sliced

1½ cups unsweetened
 almond milk

MAKES 2 (14-ounce) servings

PREP TIME 5 minutes

1. Put the pears, arugula, avocado, ginger, and almond milk in a blender. Blend on high speed until smooth.

2. Divide evenly between 2 cups and enjoy!

HEALTH HACK Add a quarter cup of chopped walnuts to boost the protein and fat.

Per serving: Calories: 243; Total Fat: 17.3g; Sugars: 9.4g; Carbohydrates: 23.4g; Fiber: 12g; Protein: 3.5g; Sodium: 128mg

Cucumber-Chia Cooler

I love the versatility of cucumbers in smoothies. Since they're mild in flavor, they are easy to sneak in without changing the flavor. Chia seeds bring an omega 3-rich punch to this refreshing cooler.

1 cup chopped cucumber, frozen

1 cup fresh spinach

1 banana, halved and frozen

2 tablespoons chia seeds

1 cup full-fat plain yogurt

1½ cups water

1. Put the cucumber, spinach, banana, chia seeds, yogurt, and water in a blender. Blend on high speed until smooth.

2. Divide evenly between 2 cups and enjoy!

Per serving: Calories: 221; Total Fat: 9.6g; Sugars: 13.4g; Carbohydrates: 28.5g; Fiber: 8.3g; Protein: 8.2g; Sodium: 97.2mg

MAKES 2 (16-ounce) servings

PREP TIME 5 minutes

SUPERCHARGE Add some freshly grated ginger for a zingy flavor, an immunity boost, and easier digestion.

Green Tea–Celery Cleanser

Green tea has been used as a medicinal food for thousands of years. Rich in protective polyphenols and antioxidants, green tea is believed to improve brain function, support weight management, and reduce cancer risk. In this cleansing smoothie, it's used as the liquid base to pair with the mineral-rich vegetables.

1 teaspoon loose-leaf green tea

½ cup boiling water

1 cup frozen pineapple chunks

1 cup chopped celery

1 cup chopped kale

1 cup coconut milk

MAKES 2 (16-ounce) servings

PREP TIME 10 minutes

SUPERCHARGE Add 2 tablespoons of chia seeds to this smoothie to boost the fiber by 8 grams.

1. Steep the green tea in the boiling water for 3 minutes. Discard the tea leaves, and then allow the tea to cool to room temperature. Alternatively, prepare the tea ahead of time and chill it in the refrigerator for up to 5 days.

2. Pour the green tea into the blender and add the pineapple, celery, kale, and coconut milk. Blend on high speed until smooth.

3. Divide evenly between 2 cups and enjoy!

Per serving: Calories: 357; Total Fat: 25.2g; Sugars: 9.1g; Carbohydrates: 25.2g; Fiber: 7.9g; Protein: 6.4g; Sodium: 73mg

Glass Full of Greens

Melon-Mint

In spring and summer, I could go for mint-flavored beverages anytime! The crispness of the apple, the sweetness of the honeydew, and the freshness of the mint leaves makes this one of my favorite summer treats. The digestion-enhancing probiotics from the kefir are just a bonus!

1 cup chopped honeydew melon, frozen

1 green apple, chopped

2 cups fresh spinach

10 mint leaves

1½ cups plain kefir

½ cup water

1. Put the melon, apple, spinach, mint, kefir, and water in a blender. Blend on high speed until smooth.

2. Divide evenly between 2 cups and enjoy!

Per serving: Calories: 185; Total Fat: 6.3g; Sugars: 22.7g; Carbohydrates: 27.1g; Fiber: 2.2g; Protein: 7.5g; Sodium: 179mg

MAKES 2 (16-ounce) servings

PREP TIME 5 minutes

SIMPLIFY To retain mint's freshness and vibrancy, simply freeze it in an airtight container, or fill an ice cube tray with water and add your mint leaves. Once frozen, transfer the mint to a freezer-safe container.

5-INGREDIENT SMOOTHIE RECIPE BOOK

Romaine Calm

Have some leftover romaine lettuce you need to use? While not often considered the healthiest of the lettuces, romaine is nutrient-rich, offering vitamins C, A, and K as well as folate, molybdenum, fiber, and iron. This easy-to-find green is also low in oxalates, offering an alternative to spinach for those prone to kidney stones.

2 cups chopped romaine lettuce

1 cup frozen strawberries

2 kiwis, peeled

¼ cup pumpkin seeds

1 cup coconut milk

MAKES 2 (14-ounce) servings

PREP TIME 5 minutes

1. Put the lettuce, strawberries, kiwis, pumpkin seeds, and coconut milk in a blender. Blend on high speed until smooth.
2. Divide evenly between 2 cups and enjoy!

SUPERCHARGE Add the juice of a lemon to this smoothie to support digestion, flush out toxins, and slow down oxidation of your smoothie.

Per serving: Calories: 345; Total Fat: 26.5g; Sugars: 12.4g; Carbohydrates: 27.9g; Fiber: 4.9g; Protein: 6.1g; Sodium: 22.4mg

Love Your Liver

Dandelion greens are nutrient-rich, acting as a great source of vitamins A, K, and C, as well as other trace minerals. These leafy greens also contain phytochemicals that have been shown to protect the liver. The combination of the greens with micronutrient-rich fruit makes this the perfect smoothie to support the body's detoxification process.

2 cups chopped
    dandelion greens
2 bananas, halved
    and frozen

2 Granny Smith apples,
    cored and chopped
1 avocado, diced and frozen
2 cups coconut water

1. Put the dandelion greens, bananas, apples, avocado, and coconut water in a blender. Blend on high speed until smooth.
2. Divide evenly between 2 cups and enjoy!

Per serving: Calories: 431; Total Fat: 16.3g; Sugars: 40.7g; Carbohydrates: 74.6g; Fiber: 18.7g; Protein: 7g; Sodium: 304mg

MAKES 2 (16-ounce) servings
PREP TIME 5 minutes

SUBSTITUTE Those taking blood thinners, such as Warfarin, may need to limit their intake of dandelion greens due to their high vitamin K levels. Swap them out for broccoli or 1 cup of cucumber, both of which contain less vitamin K.

Nectarine-Kale

Bone broth, a staple traditional food in many cultures, is making a comeback. I like to sneak this mineral-rich broth into my diet as much as possible. I often drink it straight or use it in smoothies like this one. However, I also use it as a soup base, a replacement for water when steaming rice or vegetables, or even for popsicles!

2 nectarines, chopped
and frozen
1 banana, halved and frozen
2 cups chopped kale

1 cup coconut milk yogurt
1 cup bone broth
½ cup water

MAKES 2 (16-ounce)
servings
PREP TIME 5 minutes

SIMPLIFY Freeze bananas
before they spoil. Peel
them, then break them
in half and toss them in a
freezer-safe bag.

1. Put the nectarines, banana, kale, yogurt, bone broth, and water in a blender. Blend on high speed until smooth.

2. Divide evenly between 2 cups and enjoy!

Per serving: Calories: 237; Total Fat: 6.9g; Sugars: 12.9g; Carbohydrates: 35.7g; Fiber: 4.1g; Protein: 9.6g; Sodium: 194mg

Pineapple-Pear-Parsley

While commonly used as a garnish, parsley is a nutritional powerhouse. Packed with vitamins K, C, and A, along with minerals such as calcium, iron, and folate, parsley is known for freshening breath and supporting the kidneys. Parsley carries a distinct peppery taste, so the pineapple and pear in this smoothie round out the flavor with some sweetness.

2 cups chopped chard

1 cup frozen pineapple chunks

1 pear, chopped

1 avocado, peeled and pitted

½ cup flat-leaf parsley

1½ cups water

1. Put the chard, pineapple, pear, avocado, parsley, and water in a blender. Blend on high speed until smooth.

2. Divide evenly between 2 cups and enjoy!

Per serving: Calories: 236; Total Fat: 15.1 g; Sugars: 13.4g; Carbohydrates: 27.5g; Fiber: 10.9g; Protein: 3.5g; Sodium: 54.6mg

MAKES 2 (16-ounce) servings

PREP TIME 5 minutes

SUBSTITUTE Parsley also pairs well with mango, oranges, kiwi, and coconut. Feel free to swap out the pineapple and pear for any of these fruits.

Tropi-Kale

Coconut milk has gained popularity in recent years as a dairy milk alternative. While coconuts contain a significant amount of fat, the predominant fat is lauric acid, a protective medium-chain fatty acid (MCT) that is easily absorbed by the body. During digestion, lauric acid is converted to monolaurin, a potent compound that fights pathogens such as bacteria, viruses, and yeast. Recent studies suggest that the fats from coconut do not cause detrimental changes to lipid profile, as was once believed.

1 cup frozen papaya chunks
½ cup frozen mango chunks
2 cups chopped kale
¼ cup shredded coconut
1 cup coconut milk
½ cup water

MAKES 2 (16-ounce) servings
PREP TIME 5 minutes

1. Put the papaya, mango, kale, shredded coconut, coconut milk, and water in a blender. Blend on high speed until smooth.

2. Divide evenly between 2 cups and enjoy!

Per serving: Calories: 368; Total Fat: 28.9g; Sugars: 15.3g; Carbohydrates: 29.3g; Fiber: 3.9g; Protein: 5.5g; Sodium. 76.9mg

SUPERCHARGE Add açai for a boost in nutrition. These berries are native to Brazil and are loaded with antioxidants. Açai can be found dried, in frozen fruit puree, or in powder forms.

Peachy Green

Spirulina gives this smoothie a glowing green color that will make you feel healthier just by looking at it. This blue-green algae provides a complete source of protein, containing all the essential amino acids your body requires. It's also known for its ability to help remove heavy metals from the body.

2 cups frozen sliced peaches

2 cups spring mix greens

1 avocado, peeled and pitted

2 teaspoons spirulina

1½ cups coconut water

1. Put the peaches, greens, avocado, spirulina, and coconut water in a blender. Blend on high speed until smooth.

2. Divide evenly between 2 cups and enjoy!

Per serving: Calories: 266; Total Fat: 15.7g; Sugars: 18.8g; Carbohydrates: 32g; Fiber: 11.7g; Protein: 6.1g; Sodium: 211mg

MAKES 2 (16-ounce) servings

PREP TIME 5 minutes

SUBSTITUTE Frozen raspberries, cherries, and strawberries are all great swaps for the peaches.

Spiced Apple with Spinach

Every year for Thanksgiving, I'm put in charge of the apple pie. For me, it brings back memories of being at my grandmother's house and using her old-fashioned apple peeler. I'd go extra slow as I peeled the skin to avoid breaking the long strand of green apple peel. After I finished peeling all the apples, my grandmother and I would take the long strands out to her front yard and wrap them around her tree. Then, we'd go back inside to watch the birds feast on the apple peels as the aroma of the baking apple pie wafted through the air.

2 green apples, chopped and frozen

1 cup chopped jicama

2 cups fresh spinach

2 teaspoons ground cinnamon

1½ cups unsweetened almond milk

MAKES 2 (16-ounce) servings

PREP TIME 5 minutes

1. Put the apples, jicama, spinach, cinnamon, and almond milk in a blender. Blend on high speed until smooth.
2. Divide evenly between 2 cups and enjoy!

SUPERCHARGE Add a dash of ground nutmeg for an extra note of spice and nutritional benefits. Nutmeg is great for oral health, promotes digestion, and supports the kidneys.

Per serving: Calories: 161; Total Fat: 2.8g; Sugars: 20.1g; Carbohydrates: 35.7g; Fiber: 10.1g; Protein: 2.6g; Sodium: 197mg

Detox Machine

Detoxes have become popular in recent years, and there are many harmful detox "diets" out there. Detoxification is something our bodies do daily by excreting by-products of metabolism and toxic substances we are exposed to. This process is highly nutrient-dependent, and a deficiency in any of the necessary nutrients may compromise the body's ability to detoxify. This smoothie provides nutrient-rich vegetables to aid the body in the job it's designed to do!

1 cup frozen pineapple chunks

1 banana, halved and frozen

1 cup fresh spinach

½ cup chopped broccoli

1 cup full-fat plain yogurt

1½ cups water

MAKES 2 (16-ounce) servings

PREP TIME 5 minutes

1. Put the pineapple, banana, spinach, broccoli, yogurt, and water in a blender. Blend on high speed until smooth.

2. Divide evenly between 2 cups and enjoy!

SUPERCHARGE Parsley, which supports the body's detoxification process, would make a great addition to this detox smoothie.

Per serving: Calories: 209; Total Fat: 6.4g; Sugars: 15.3g; Carbohydrates: 25.9g; Fiber: 2.7g; Protein: 12g; Sodium: 90.1mg

Sweet Pepper

Bell peppers, also called sweet peppers, can make an unexpectedly pleasant addition to your smoothie. This pepper is 92 percent water and rich in nutrients such as vitamin C, beta-carotene, and folate. Green bell peppers are unripe and will be the most bitter, while red, yellow, and orange ones will be sweeter.

2 oranges, peeled, portioned, and frozen

2 cups fresh spinach

1 yellow bell pepper, chopped

1 cup full-fat plain yogurt

1½ cups coconut water

1. Put the oranges, spinach, bell pepper, yogurt, and coconut water in a blender. Blend on high speed until smooth.

2. Divide evenly between 2 cups and enjoy!

Per serving: Calories: 204; Total Fat: 4.8g; Sugars: 24.8g; Carbohydrates: 35.1g; Fiber: 6.3g; Protein: 8.3g; Sodium: 322mg

MAKES 2 (14-ounce) servings

PREP TIME 5 minutes

KID FRIENDLY If you think your child won't be willing to try a bell pepper smoothie, substitute the yellow bell pepper with one cup of guava, which is also high in vitamin C.

Pineapple-Papaya-Cactus

The nopal cactus, also known as the prickly pear cactus, is commonly consumed as a vegetable in some regions in Mexico and the Southwestern United States. While the pads are rich in fiber, antioxidants, B vitamins, and vitamin C, the juice from the leaves is also known for its anti-inflammatory and immune-boosting properties. Fresh, canned, and pickled nopal cacti are readily available in many grocery stores.

½ cup frozen
  pineapple chunks
½ cup frozen papaya chunks
1 cup diced fresh cactus
  (nopales), spines removed

2 tablespoons chia seeds
1 cup coconut milk
½ cup water

MAKES 2 (14-ounce) servings
PREP TIME 5 minutes

SUBSTITUTE If you are unable to find cactus, replace it with 2 cups of leafy greens or chopped cucumbers.

1. Put the pineapple, papaya, cactus, chia seeds, coconut milk, and water in a blender. Blend on high speed until smooth.

2. Divide evenly between 2 cups and enjoy!

Per serving: Calories: 349; Total Fat: 29.6g; Sugars: 6.6g; Carbohydrates: 21.1g; Fiber: 8.8g; Protein: 6g; Sodium: 28.5mg

Sea Breeze

This is my go-to smoothie when I am craving a beach vacation. As I'm sipping this tropical drink, I imagine myself lounging in a hammock on the beach while smelling the salty breeze. I can dream, can't I?

1 cup frozen pineapple chunks

½ cup frozen mango chunks

2 cups fresh spinach

2 teaspoons spirulina powder

1 cup coconut milk

½ cup water

1. Put the pineapple, mango, spinach, spirulina powder, coconut milk, and water in a blender. Blend on high speed until smooth.

2. Divide evenly between 2 cups and enjoy!

Per serving: Calories: 305; Total Fat: 24.6g; Sugars: 14.3g; Carbohydrates: 23g; Fiber: 2g; Protein: 5.1g; Sodium: 113mg

MAKES 2 (16-ounce) servings

PREP TIME 5 minutes

HEALTH HACK Boost the protein in this smoothie with a tablespoon of sunflower seed butter.

DRINKABLE DESSERTS

Orange Dreamsicle

As a child, when the ice-cream truck came to my neighborhood, you could always find me lined up, ready to order an orange creamsicle. This smoothie is my healthy rendition of one of my favorite frozen treats and includes a bonus orange vegetable. When dessert includes a veggie, there's no shame in enjoying something sweet for breakfast!

2 oranges, peeled

1 banana, halved and frozen

½ cup chopped carrots

¼ cup raw cashews

½ cup coconut milk

1 cup water

MAKES 2 (14-ounce) servings

PREP TIME 5 minutes

1. Put the oranges, banana, carrots, cashews, coconut milk, and water in a blender. Blend on high speed until smooth.

2. Divide evenly between 2 cups and enjoy!

KID FRIENDLY Using a ripe banana will already sweeten this smoothie, but if you want it a bit sweeter still, add a little honey.

Per serving: Calories: 265; Total Fat: 14g; Sugars: 21.1g; Carbohydrates: 36.9g; Fiber: 5.8g; Protein: 3.9g; Sodium: 39mg

Strawberry Cheesecake

Cottage cheese offers not only a dense source of protein but also the slightly tangy taste of cheesecake in this smoothie. Fold in some cacao nibs after blending for a dark chocolate variety. For a different berry flavor, swap the strawberries with some blueberries or raspberries.

2 cups frozen strawberries
½ cup full-fat cottage cheese
2 pitted dates

3 tablespoons hulled hemp seeds
½ cup full-fat plain yogurt
1½ cups water

1. Put the strawberries, cottage cheese, dates, hemp seeds, yogurt, and water in a blender. Blend on high speed until smooth.

2. Divide evenly between 2 cups and enjoy!

Per serving: Calories: 293; Total Fat: 11.9g; Sugars: 27.7g; Carbohydrates: 35.4g; Fiber: 4.6g; Protein: 14.9g; Sodium: 236mg

MAKES 2 (16-ounce) servings
PREP TIME 5 minutes

SUPERCHARGE Add 1 teaspoon of camu camu powder to give this smoothie a healthy dose of vitamin C. Camu camu, a South American fruit, offers 760 percent of the daily recommended intake of vitamin C in just one teaspoon. Camu camu powder can be found at many health food stores or online.

Drinkable Desserts

Lemon Tart

During my last pregnancy, I craved everything lemon, and thus, this smoothie was born. Turmeric gives this smoothie its lemon-yellow color. Top it with some whipped cream or whipped coconut cream for a fun, fluffy topping. You can even give this smoothie a vacation vibe by adding chopped frozen mango and coconut flakes.

1 lemon, peeled

2 bananas, halved and frozen

2 tablespoons chia seeds

1 teaspoon ground turmeric

1 cup full-fat plain yogurt

1½ cups water

1. Put the lemon, bananas, chia seeds, turmeric, yogurt, and water in a blender. Blend on high speed until smooth.

2. Divide evenly between 2 cups and enjoy!

Per serving: Calories: 300; Total Fat: 10.2g; Sugars: 22.8g; Carbohydrates: 50.9g; Fiber: 12.8g; Protein: 9.5g; Sodium: 63.3mg

MAKES 2 (16-ounce) servings

PREP TIME 5 minutes

SUBSTITUTE To make this smoothie into a "lime tart," swap the lemon and turmeric with a lime and use a handful of spinach for the green color.

Peach Cobbler

Dating back to the 1850s, cobbler has been considered a staple dessert in American cooking. Depending on what your heart desires, you can substitute other popular fruits, such as blackberries, apples, or cherries, for the peaches. You can even add some whipped coconut cream for extra decadence.

2 cups frozen sliced peaches

½ cup rolled oats

½ teaspoon ground cinnamon

2 tablespoons ground flaxseed

1½ cups unsweetened almond milk

MAKES 2 (14-ounce) servings

PREP TIME 5 minutes

KID FRIENDLY Sprinkle some granola on top to resemble a cobbler dough topping.

1. Put the peaches, oats, cinnamon, flaxseed, and almond milk in a blender. Blend on high speed until smooth.

2. Divide evenly between 2 cups and enjoy!

Per serving: Calories: 277; Total Fat: 8.3g; Sugars: 13g; Carbohydrates: 44.3g; Fiber: 7.4g; Protein: 10g; Sodium: 123mg

Drinkable Desserts

Double Chocolate Chip

Calling all chocolate lovers! There's no guilt in eating chocolate when it's pure and high in antioxidants, polyphenols, flavanols, and other health-promoting compounds. No wonder the Incas considered it the drink of the gods! Cacao nibs, which are fragments of cacao beans, provide a bit of crunch to this dark chocolate smoothie.

2 bananas, halved and frozen

1 avocado, peeled and pitted

1 tablespoon raw cacao powder

1½ cups unsweetened almond milk

2 tablespoons cacao nibs

MAKES 2 (12-ounce) servings

PREP TIME 5 minutes

HEALTH HACK Add 2 tablespoons of nut butter in step one to increase the protein content by 4 grams per serving.

1. Put the bananas, avocado, cacao powder, and almond milk in a blender. Blend on high speed until smooth.

2. Add the cacao nibs to the blender bowl. Using a spatula, fold them into the smoothie until combined.

3. Divide evenly between 2 cups and enjoy!

Per serving: Calories: 263; Total Fat: 24.7g; Sugars: 0.8g; Carbohydrates: 15g; Fiber: 10.7g; Protein: 5.1g; Sodium: 131mg

Pomegranate Sorbet

Blending frozen fruit with a banana and yogurt results in a delicious, refreshing, no-added-sugar treat! I like to use pomegranate seeds and raspberries to round out the flavor, but you can get creative with the fruits for this sorbet. Apricot, mango, pink grapefruit, orange, and watermelon would work well with this recipe.

1½ cups frozen pomegranate seeds

½ cup frozen raspberries

1 banana, halved and frozen

1 tablespoon chia seeds

1 cup full-fat plain yogurt

1½ cups water

MAKES 2 (16-ounce) servings

PREP TIME 5 minutes

SUBSTITUTE Make this smoothie dairy-free by using coconut milk instead of yogurt.

1. Put the pomegranate seeds, raspberries, banana, chia seeds, yogurt, and water in a blender. Blend on high speed until smooth.

2. Divide evenly between 2 cups and enjoy!

Per serving: Calories: 266; Total Fat: 7.1 g; Sugars: 29.3g; Carbohydrates: 49g, Fiber: 12.7g; Protein: 7g; Sodium: 35mg

Pistachio Cream

Turn to this recipe to make yourself some no-churn pistachio ice cream! Using raw pistachios will provide a cleaner flavor and a greener green than roasted pistachios. If you want to add a bit of crunch to your treat, fold in a quarter cup of roughly chopped pistachios before serving. I love eating mine in a bowl with a spoon to heighten the ice-cream experience!

⅓ cup raw pistachios
1 banana, halved and frozen
½ avocado, chopped
    and frozen

1 teaspoon vanilla extract
1½ cups unsweetened
    almond milk

MAKES 2 (12-ounce) servings
PREP TIME 5 minutes

SUPERCHARGE To enhance the green color in this smoothie even more, add a dash of spirulina.

1. Put the pistachios, banana, avocado, vanilla, and almond milk in a blender. Blend on high speed until smooth.

2. Divide evenly between 2 cups and enjoy!

Per serving: Calories: 272; Total Fat: 18.8g; Sugars: 9.1g; Carbohydrates: 24.2g; Fiber: 7.7g; Protein: 6.6g; Sodium: 124mg

Caramel-Covered Apple

This smoothie is a healthier version of the famous fall festival treat, and it won't get stuck in your teeth! You'll be surprised to find how much the combination of dates and cashews bring out the caramel flavor. If you can't find pitted dates, be sure to slice them lengthwise and pop out the small pit inside before tossing them into your smoothie. Additionally, I use a bit of collagen powder in this smoothie for a boost in protein, but for a vegetarian option, feel free to use a plant-based protein powder instead.

2 apples, chopped
   and frozen
2 pitted dates
¼ cup raw cashews

2 tablespoons
   collagen powder
1½ cups unsweetened
   almond milk

MAKES 2 (14-ounce) servings
PREP TIME 5 minutes

1. Put the apples, dates, cashews, collagen powder, and almond milk in a blender. Blend on high speed until smooth.

2. Divide evenly between 2 cups and enjoy!

Per serving: Calories: 300; Total Fat: 8.7g; Sugars: 35.7g; Carbohydrates: 48.5g; Fiber: 7.2g; Protein: 13.2g; Sodium: 179mg

SIMPLIFY Dried dates can be frozen. Just remove their pits, put the dates in an airtight container, and pop them into the freezer. Sugar crystals may appear beneath the skin, but they will not affect their taste or nutritional qualities.

Drinkable Desserts

Pumpkin Chai

"Chai" is the Hindi word for "tea." Recipes vary, but this spiced tea is traditionally made using a combination of black tea and aromatic warming spices, such as cinnamon, cardamom, cloves, ginger, and black pepper. Chai is traditionally brewed using warm milk, and then lightly sweetened. For this chilled smoothie adaptation, we are using pumpkin spice blend as a shortcut, which commonly features cinnamon, ginger, and nutmeg.

½ cup pumpkin puree

1 banana, halved and frozen

½ teaspoon pumpkin
  spice blend

1 teaspoon vanilla extract

1½ cups unsweetened
  almond milk

MAKES 2 (12-ounce) servings

PREP TIME 5 minutes

SIMPLIFY Freeze pumpkin puree in an ice cube tray for quick use in smoothies.

1. Put the pumpkin puree, banana, pumpkin spice blend, vanilla, and almond milk in a blender. Blend on high speed until smooth.

2. Divide evenly between 2 cups and enjoy!

Per serving: Calories: 157; Total Fat: 5.6g; Sugars: 7.5g; Carbohydrates: 23.3g; Fiber: 2.3g; Protein: 4.4g; Sodium: 124mg

Raspberries and White Chocolate

Coconut butter is coconut meat that has been ground up and processed until smooth, like a nut butter. It carries a naturally sweet taste that combines beautifully with vanilla for a sugar-free white chocolate flavor. We're using raspberries in this recipe, but give strawberries, pineapple, or cherries a try, too!

1 cup frozen raspberries

1 banana, halved and frozen

2 tablespoons
  coconut butter

½ teaspoon vanilla extract

1½ cups milk

MAKES 2 (12-ounce) servings

PREP TIME 5 minutes

SUPERCHARGE For a ruby-red color and extra health benefits, add beet root powder.

1. Put the raspberries, banana, coconut butter, vanilla, and milk in a blender. Blend on high speed until smooth.

2. Divide evenly between 2 cups and enjoy!

Per serving: Calories: 256; Total Fat: 14.7g; Sugars: 17.2g; Carbohydrates: 25.4g; Fiber: 1.5g; Protein: 7.1g; Sodium: 72.9mg

Drinkable Desserts

Banana-Zucchini Bread

One of my fondest memories as a child was the sweet aroma of banana bread baking in the oven. This grain-free version takes me back to my younger days. Add some nut butter, shredded coconut, or chia seeds for more variety.

1 cup chopped zucchini

2 bananas, halved and frozen

¼ cup walnuts

½ teaspoon ground cinnamon

1 cup full-fat plain yogurt

1½ cups water

1. Put the zucchini, bananas, walnuts, cinnamon, yogurt, and water in a blender. Blend on high speed until smooth.

2. Divide evenly between 2 cups and enjoy!

Per serving: Calories: 287; Total Fat: 14g; Sugars: 21.6g; Carbohydrates: 37.2g; Fiber: 5.1g; Protein: 8.5g; Sodium: 64.1mg

MAKES 2 (16-ounce) servings

PREP TIME 5 minutes

HEALTH HACK Add ½ cup of rolled oats to bulk up this smoothie.

Layered Berries and Cream

This lavishly layered smoothie takes a few extra steps to create the layers separately, but the effort makes for an ultra-luscious experience. The key is to have the smoothie mixtures thick enough so that they won't blend together when you pour them. For variety, try this smoothie with a different colored fruit layer by using either mangos or cherries. You could even add some color to the white layer by adding cacao powder or spirulina.

1 cup full-fat plain Greek yogurt

1 teaspoon honey

½ teaspoon vanilla extract

1½ cups whole milk, divided

2 cups frozen mixed berries

MAKES 2 (16-ounce) servings

PREP TIME 5 minutes

SUBSTITUTE Substitute canned coconut milk for the whole milk for a thicker consistency in the layers.

1. **To prepare the bottom cream layer:** Put the yogurt, honey, vanilla, and ½ cup of milk in a blender. Blend on high speed until smooth.

2. Divide the "cream" evenly between 2 cups. Set aside.

3. **To prepare the berry layer:** Put the mixed berries and remaining 1 cup of milk in the blender. Blend on high speed until smooth.

4. Pour the berry layer carefully over the cream layer, dividing evenly between 2 cups. Enjoy!

Per serving: Calories: 238; Total Fat: 9.9g; Sugars: 24.9g; Carbohydrates: 29.2g; Fiber: 3g; Protein: 10.7g; Sodium: 125mg

Cherry Pudding

Vegetables for dessert? You betcha! I promise you won't even notice the cauliflower in this indulgent smoothie. I use coconut butter to sneak in all the benefits of raw coconut while adding a touch of natural sweetness. Add some cacao powder for a decadent dark chocolate and cherry pudding.

1 cup frozen pitted cherries

1 cup frozen
  cauliflower florets

1 cup full-fat plain yogurt

1 tablespoon coconut butter
  (or coconut manna)

1½ cups whole milk

MAKES 2 (16-ounce) servings

PREP TIME 5 minutes

1. Put the cherries, cauliflower, yogurt, coconut butter, and milk in a blender. Blend on high speed until smooth.

2. Divide evenly between 2 cups and enjoy!

SIMPLIFY Coconut butter can be difficult to scoop from the container when solid. To loosen it up, put the jar in a bowl with hot water for about 10 minutes, then scoop.

Per serving: Calories: 274; Total Fat: 14.3g; Sugars: 23.2g; Carbohydrates: 27.2g; Fiber: 2.5g; Protein: 11.9g; Sodium: 142mg

Eggnog

Eggnog was my favorite holiday beverage as a child. Now that I have kids of my own, I want to pass along the same tradition. With this smoothie, we can enjoy the holiday treat without the sugar hit.

2 bananas, halved and frozen

2 pitted dates

½ teaspoon ground nutmeg

½ teaspoon ground cinnamon

1½ cups unsweetened almond milk

1. Put the bananas, dates, nutmeg, cinnamon, and almond milk in a blender. Blend on high speed until smooth.

2. Divide evenly between 2 cups and enjoy!

Per serving: Calories: 202; Total Fat: 2.9g; Sugars: 30.5g; Carbohydrates: 46.4g; Fiber: 5.9g; Protein: 2.5g; Sodium: 122mg

MAKES 2 (14-ounce) servings

PREP TIME 5 minutes

HEALTH HACK Increase the protein for a more filling beverage by adding a cup of yogurt.

Drinkable Desserts

Butter Pecan

My husband's favorite ice-cream is butter pecan, so I knew the way to his heart would be to recreate a healthy smoothie version. Butternut squash adds a mild sweetness, along with fiber and vitamins A and C. We're using it raw in this smoothie for simplicity, but if you have some leftover cooked butternut squash, it makes for an even dreamier, velvety consistency!

½ cup frozen butternut squash chunks

1 banana, halved and frozen

2 pitted dates

¼ cup pecans

1½ cups unsweetened almond milk

MAKES 2 (16-ounce) servings

PREP TIME 5 minutes

1. Put the squash, banana, dates, pecans, and almond milk in a blender. Blend on high speed until smooth.

2. Divide evenly between 2 cups and enjoy!

SIMPLIFY Purchase frozen butternut squash in the frozen foods aisle at your grocery store.

Per serving: Calories: 255; Total Fat: 12.3g; Sugars: 24.5g; Carbohydrates: 38.2g; Fiber: 5.9g; Protein: 3.4g; Sodium: 122mg

Measurement Conversions

	US STANDARD	US STANDARD (OUNCES)	METRIC (APPROXIMATE)
VOLUME EQUIVALENTS (LIQUID)	2 tablespoons	1 fl. oz.	30 mL
	¼ cup	2 fl. oz.	60 mL
	½ cup	4 fl. oz.	120 mL
	1 cup	8 fl. oz.	240 mL
	1½ cups	12 fl. oz.	355 mL
	2 cups or 1 pint	16 fl. oz.	475 mL
	4 cups or 1 quart	32 fl. oz.	1 L
	1 gallon	128 fl. oz.	4 L
VOLUME EQUIVALENTS (DRY)	⅛ teaspoon	——————	0.5 mL
	¼ teaspoon	——————	1 mL
	½ teaspoon	——————	2 mL
	¾ teaspoon	——————	4 mL
	1 teaspoon	——————	5 mL
	1 tablespoon	——————	15 mL
	¼ cup	——————	59 mL
	⅓ cup	——————	79 mL
	½ cup	——————	118 mL
	⅔ cup	——————	156 mL
	¾ cup	——————	177 mL
	1 cup	——————	235 mL
	2 cups or 1 pint	——————	475 mL
	3 cups	——————	700 mL
	4 cups or 1 quart	——————	1 L
	½ gallon	——————	2 L
	1 gallon	——————	4 L
WEIGHT EQUIVALENTS	½ ounce	——————	15 g
	1 ounce	——————	30 g
	2 ounces	——————	60 g
	4 ounces	——————	115 g
	8 ounces	——————	225 g
	12 ounces	——————	340 g
	16 ounces or 1 pound	——————	455 g

	FAHRENHEIT (F)	CELSIUS (C) (APPROXIMATE)
OVEN TEMPERATURES	250°F	120°C
	300°F	150°C
	325°F	180°C
	375°F	190°C
	400°F	200°C
	425°F	220°C
	450°F	230°C

References

Abourashed, E. A., and A. T. El-Alfy. "Chemical Diversity and Pharmacological Significance of the Secondary Metabolites of Nutmeg (*Myristica Fragrans* Houtt)." *Phytochemistry Reviews: Proceedings of the Phytochemical Society of Europe* 15, no. 6 (December 2016): 1035–56. doi.org/10.1007/s11101-016-9469-x.

Ashokkumar, K., et al. "Botany, Traditional Uses, Phytochemistry and Biological Activities of Cardamom [Elettaria cardamomum (L.) Maton]—A Critical review." *Journal of Ethnopharmacology* 246 (September 2019). doi.org/10.1016/j.jep.2019.112244.

Asserin, Jerome, et al. "The Effect of Oral Collagen Peptide Supplementation on Skin Moisture and the Dermal Collagen Network: Evidence From an Ex Vivo Model and Randomized, Placebo-Controlled Clinical Trials." *Journal of Cosmetic Dermatology* 14, no. 4 (September 2015): 291–301. doi.org/10.1111/jocd.12174.

Bashir, Khawaja M. I., and Jae-Suk Choi. "Clinical and Physiological Perspectives of B-Glucans: The Past, Present, and Future." *International Journal of Molecular Sciences* 18, no. 9 (September 2017): 1906. doi.org/10.3390/ijms18091906.

Bello, Alfonso E., and Steffen Oesser. "Collagen Hydrolysate for the Treatment of Osteoarthritis and Other Joint Disorders: a Review of the Literature." *Current Medical Research and Opinion* 22, no. 11 (November 2006): 2221-32. doi:10.1185/030079906X148373.

Bowman, Barbara. "Nopales (Nopalitos)." Gourmet Sleuth. Accessed September 2, 2020. GourmetSleuth.com/articles/detail/nopalitos.

Carr, Anitra C., and Silvia Maggini. "Vitamin C and Immune Function." *Nutrients* 9, no. 11 (November 2017): 1211. doi:10.3390/nu9111211.

Clinton, S. K. "Lycopene: Chemistry, Biology, and Implications for Human Health and Disease." *Nutrition Reviews* 56, no. 2 Pt 1 (February 1998): 35–51. doi.org/10.1111/j.1753-4887.1998.tb01691.x.

De Oliveira, J. R., S. Camargo, and L. D. de Oliveira. "Rosmarinus Officinalis L. (Rosemary) as Therapeutic and Prophylactic Agent." *Journal of Biomedical Science* 26, no. 1 (January 2019): 5. doi.org/10.1186/s12929-019-0499-8.

Ekanayaka R. A., et al. "Impact of a Traditional Dietary Supplement with Coconut Milk and Soya Milk on the Lipid Profile in Normal Free Living Subjects." *Journal of Nutrition and Metabolism* 2013 (October 2013). doi:10.1155/2013/481068.

Farzaei, M. H., et al. "Parsley: A Review of Ethnopharmacology, Phytochemistry and Biological Activities." *Journal of Traditional Chinese Medicine* 33, no. 6 (December 2013): 815–26. doi.org/10.1016/s0254-6272(14)60018-2.

Ferreira, Mandy. "Fifteen Health Benefits of Pomegranate Juice." Medical News Today. Accessed August 24, 2020. MedicalNewsToday.com/articles/318385.

Gunnars, Kris. "6 Health Benefits of Apple Cider Vinegar Backed by Science." Heathline. Accessed September 2, 2020. HealthLine.com/nutrition/6-proven-health-benefits-of-apple-cider-vinegar.

He, Jian, and M. Monica Giusti. "Anthocyanins: Natural Colorants with Health-Promoting Properties." *Annual Review of Food Science and Technology*, 1 (2010): 163–87. doi.org/10.1146/annurev.food.080708.100754.

Hu, Jiang, D. Webster, J. Cao, and A. Shao. "The Safety of Green Tea and Green Tea Extract Consumption in Adults—Results of a Systematic Review." *Regulatory Toxicology and Pharmacology* 95 (June 2018). doi.org/10.1016/j.yrtph.2018.03.019.

Jurenka, Julie S. "Anti-inflammatory properties of curcumin, a major constituent of Curcuma longa: a review of preclinical and clinical research." *Alternative Medicine* 14, no. 2 (September 2009): 141–53. PMID: 19594223.

Kahathuduwa, Chanaka N., et al. "Acute Effects of Theanine, Caffeine and Theanine-Caffeine Combination on Attention." *Nutritional Neuroscience* 20, no. 6 (February 2017): 369–77. doi.org/10.1080/1028415X.2016.1144845.

Kaltenberg, Jennifer, et al. "Zinc Signals Promote IL-2-Dependent Proliferation of T Cells." *European Journal of Immunology* 40, no. 5 (April 2010): 1496–503. doi.org/10.1002/eji.200939574.

Kelley, Darshan S., Yuriko Adkins, and Kevin D. Laugero. "A Review of the Health Benefits of Cherries." *Nutrients* 10, no. 3 (March 2018): 368. doi.org/10.3390/nu10030368.

Linus Pauling Institute. "Cruciferous Vegetables." Oregon State University. Accessed August 29, 2020. LPI.OregonState.edu/mic/food-beverages/cruciferous-vegetables.

Linus Pauling Institute. "Essential Fatty Acids." Oregon State University. Accessed
    August 29, 2020. LPI.OregonState.edu/mic/other-nutrients/essential-fatty-acids.

Linus Pauling Institute. "Lignans." Oregon State University. Accessed August 29, 2020.
    LPI.OregonState.edu/mic/dietary-factors/phytochemicals/lignans.

McCulloch, Marsha. "Cacao vs. Cocoa: What's the Difference." Healthline. Accessed
    August 25, 2020. HealthLine.com/nutrition/cacao-vs-cocoa.

Misbahuddin, M., et al. "Efficacy of Spirulina Extract Plus Zinc in Patients of Chronic Arse-
    nic Poisoning: A Randomized Placebo-Controlled Study." *Clinical Toxicology 44, no.* 2
    (2006): 135–41. doi.org/10.1080/15563650500514400.

Morgano, Marcelo A., et al. "Determination of Water Content in Brazilian
    Honeybee-Collected Pollen by Karl Fischer Titration." *Food Control* 22, no. 10 (March
    2011): 1604–08. doi.org/10.1016/j.foodcont.2011.03.016.

Nugent, A. P. "Health Properties of Resistant Starch." *Nutrition Bulletin* 30, no. 1 (February
    2005): 27–54. doi.org/10.1111/j.1467-3010.2005.00481.x.

Petre, Alina. "10 Benefits of Golden (Turmeric) Milk and How to Make it." Healthline.
    Accessed August 25, 2020. HealthLine.com/nutrition/golden-milk-turmeric#section2.

Rao, Pasupuleti Visweswara, and Siew Hua Gan. "Cinnamon: A Multifaceted Medicinal
    Plant." *Evidence Based Complementary Alternative Medicine* 2014 (April 2014).
    Epub doi.org/10.1155/2014/642942.

Rennard, B. O., et al. "Chicken Soup Inhibits Neutrophil Chemotaxis in Vitro." *Chest* 118, no.
    4 (October 2000): 1150–57. doi.org/10.1378/chest.118.4.1150.

Round, June L., and Sarkis K. Mazmanian. "The Gut Microbiota Shapes Intestinal Immune
    Responses During Health and Disease." *Nature Reviews. Immunology* 9, no.5 (May 2009):
    313–23. doi.org/10.1038/nri2515.

Semwal, Ruchi Badoni, et al. "Gingerols and Shogaols: Important Nutraceutical
    Principles From Ginger." *Phytochemistry* 117 (September 2015): 554–68. doi:10.1016/j
    .phytochem.2015.07.012.

Strandwitz, Philip. "Neurotransmitter Modulation by the Gut Microbiota." *Brain Research*
    1693, Part B (August 2018): 128–33. doi:10.1016/j.brainres.2018.03.015.

References

130

Subash, Selvaraju, et al. "Neuroprotective Effects of Berry Fruits on Neurodegenerative Diseases." *Neural Regeneration Research* 9, no. 16, (August 2014): 1557–66. doi.org/10.4103/1673-5374.139483.

USDA Agricultural Research Service. "FoodData Central Search Results: Avocado, Raw." USDA. Accessed August 22, 2020. ndb.nal.USDA.gov/fdc-app.html#/food-details /786651/nutrients.

USDA Agricultural Research Service. "FoodData Central Search Results: Banana, Raw." USDA. Accessed August 22, 2020. ndb.nal.USDA.gov/fdc app.html#/food-details /786652/nutrients.

USDA Agricultural Research Service. "FoodData Central Search Results: Bone Broth." USDA. Accessed August 29, 2020. ndb.nal.USDA.gov/fdc-app.html#/food-details /551729/nutrients.

USDA Agricultural Research Service. "FoodData Central Search Results: Camu Camu Powder." USDA. Accessed September 1, 2020. ndb.nal.USDA.gov/fdc-app.html# /food-details/1065723/nutrients.

USDA Agricultural Research Service. "FoodData Central Search Results: Cantaloupe, Raw." USDA. Accessed August 23, 2020. ndb.nal.USDA.gov/fdc-app.html#/food-details /786661/nutrients.

USDA Agricultural Research Service. "FoodData Central Search Results: Chia Seeds." USDA. Accessed August 23, 2020. ndb.nal.USDA.gov/fdc-app.html#/food-details /784468/nutrients.

USDA Agricultural Research Service. "FoodData Central Search Results: Collards, Raw." USDA. Accessed September 1, 2020. ndb.nal.USDA.gov/fdc-app.html#/food-details /787220/nutrients.

USDA Agricultural Research Service. "FoodData Central Search Results: Dandelion Greens, Raw." USDA. Accessed September 3, 2020. ndb.nal.USDA.gov/fdc-app.html# /food-details/787264/nutrients.

USDA Agricultural Research Service. "FoodData Central Search Results: Guava, Raw." USDA. Accessed September 8, 2020. ndb.nal.USDA.gov/fdc-app.html#/food-details /786690/nutrients.

USDA Agricultural Research Service. "FoodData Central Search Results: Jicama, Raw."
USDA. Accessed August 24, 2020. fdc.nal.USDA.gov/fdc-app.html#/food-details
/787794/nutrients.

USDA Agricultural Research Service. "FoodData Central Search Results: Nopales, Raw."
USDA. Accessed September 2, 2020. ndb.nal.USDA.gov/fdc-app.html#/food-details
/168571/nutrients.

USDA Agricultural Research Service. "FoodData Central Search Results: Parsley, Raw."
USDA. Accessed September 1, 2020. ndb.nal.usda.gov/fdc-app.html#/food-details
/787805/nutrients.

USDA Agricultural Research Service. "FoodData Central Search Results: Parsnips, Raw."
USDA. Accessed August 22, 2020. ndb.nal.USDA.gov/fdc-app.html#/food-details
/170417/nutrients.

USDA Agricultural Research Service. "FoodData Central Search Results: Peppers, Sweet,
Yellow, Raw." USDA. Accessed September 1, 2020. ndb.nal.USDA.gov/fdc-app.html#
/food-details/169383/nutrients.

USDA Agricultural Research Service. "FoodData Central Search Results: Pumpkin, Raw."
USDA. Accessed August 22, 2020. ndb.nal.USDA.gov/fdc-app.html#/food-details
/168448/nutrients.

USDA Agricultural Research Service. "FoodData Central Search Results: Quinoa, Cooked."
USDA. Accessed August 27, 2020. ndb.nal.USDA.gov/fdc-app.html#/food-details
/168917/nutrients.

USDA Agricultural Research Service. "FoodData Central Search Results: Radishes, Raw."
USDA. Accessed August 22, 2020. fdc.nal.USDA.gov/fdc-app.html#/food-details
/169276/nutrients.

USDA Agricultural Research Service. "FoodData Central Search Results: Romaine Lettuce,
Raw." USDA. Accessed September 3, 2020. ndb.nal.USDA.gov/fdc-app.html#/food-details
/787271/nutrients.

USDA Agricultural Research Service. "FoodData Central Search Results: Seeds, Flaxseed."
USDA. Accessed August 22, 2020. ndb.nal.USDA.gov/fdc-app.html#/food-details
/169414/nutrients.

USDA Agricultural Research Service. "FoodData Central Search Results: Seeds, Hemp Seeds, Hulled." USDA. Accessed August 22, 2020. ndb.nal.USDA.gov/fdc-app.html# /food-details/170148/nutrients.

USDA Agricultural Research Service. "FoodData Central Search Results: Squash, Winter, Butternut, Raw." USDA. Accessed September 4, 2020. ndb.nal.USDA.gov/fdc-app.html# /food-details/169295/nutrients.

USDA Agricultural Research Service. "FoodData Central Search Results: Zucchini, Raw." USDA. Accessed September 2, 2020. ndb.nal.usda.gov/fdc-app.html#/food-details /595040/nutrients.

Ware, Megan. "The Health Benefits of Cayenne Pepper." Medical News Today. Accessed August 27, 2020. MedicalNewsToday.com/articles/267248.

Yu-Yahiro J. A. "Electrolytes and Their Relationship to Normal and Abnormal Muscle Function." *Orthopedic Nursing 13*, no. 5 (September 1994): 38–40. doi.org/10.1097 /00006416-199409000-00008.

Index

Index

Index

Acknowledgments

First and foremost, I thank God for these wholesome foods that provide nourishment to our bodies. It's these whole foods that support our health and healing.

My smoothies would still be tucked away on scratch paper in a drawer somewhere if it wasn't for the team that helped me bring them to life. For that, I'd like to show my gratitude to everyone on the Callisto team. Special thanks to Van and Alyssa, my ever-patient editors, and Kate Sears, who gave the smoothies their glamour shots, as well as Sara Feinstein, the photo manager, and Mando Daniel, the designer.

I'm eternally grateful to my husband, Andrew, for always believing in me and keeping our house running when I had to hide away in the office to write. I'd like to thank my sons, Jude and Luke, who were the best recipe testers—always giving their 100 percent downright honest, uninhibited feedback on my smoothie creations.

My deepest appreciation goes to my parents, David and Linda, for their unwavering love, support, and encouragement to never stop dreaming. My heartfelt thanks to my mother-in-law, Irma, who never hesitated to help watch the boys while I worked.

Thank you all from the bottom of my heart.

About the Author

Amy Gonzalez is a registered dietitian and functional nutrition therapy practitioner. She specializes in women's health and uses an approach that combines real foods, mindful eating, and functional nutrition. She works with clients one-on-one and leads an online group sugar detox program. Amy lives in Fort Worth, Texas, with her husband and two sons, who are her official taste-testers. In her spare time, you can find her tending to her flock of backyard chickens or out with her sons discovering new nature trails. You can find Amy on her website (TheHolisticRD.com) or on Instagram @The.Holistic.Dietitian.